# Offshoring Strategies

# Offshoring Strategies

## Evolving Captive Center Models

Ilan Oshri

The MIT Press
Cambridge, Massachusetts
London, England

For information about special quantity discounts, please e-mail special_sales@mitpress.mit.edu

This book was set in Palatino by Toppan Best-set Premedia Limited. Printed and bound in the United States of America.

Library of Congress Cataloging-in-Publication Data

Oshri, Ilan.
Offshoring strategies: evolving captive center models / Ilan Oshri.
    p.  cm.
Includes bibliographical references and index.
ISBN 978-0-262-01560-8 (alk. paper)
1. Offshore outsourcing.  2. Subsidiary corporations.  I. Title.
HD2365.0825   2011
658.4'058—dc22

                                                              2010036053

10   9   8   7   6   5   4   3   2   1

# Contents

# Foreword

As our economy continues its march toward globalization, companies are constantly exploring new and better ways to both reach local markets with their products and services and to leverage the skills, talents, and resources they find there to improve their own operations. Outsourcing, offshoring, and shared services are all part of this phenomenon.

As a result of these experiences, the range of approaches available to companies today is extensive. But closing the gap between pursuing any particular approach and getting it right is quite simply the difference between success and failure.

Captive centers are no exception. As Ilan Oshri points in this excellent book, in the last fifteen years more than 50 percent of Fortune 250 companies have set up hundreds of captive centers around the globe. But, based on his extensive research and case study development, many of them have struggled, and those that do not struggle often do not have a clear strategic roadmap to make them successful in the long term.

This does not have to be the case. When done right, captive centers can add tremendous value to an organization and even evolve from simply providing services to their parent firm to become a center of excellence and a source for profit. This has been the result for many companies. In some cases, what begins as a small captive center turns into the cornerstone of a global shared services operations. In others, companies build on the value created by commercializing their high-powered internal operations. Genpact, one of the world's most successful outsourcing companies, was originally GE's captive center in India. Today, Genpact serves hundreds of customers around the world and delivers both world-class services and investment returns to its former parent. Similarly, WNS began as part of British Airways. In fact, many of today's outsourcing companies began as the specialized unit of a parent company. Companies like Convergys, Delphi, and First Data began as part of Cincinnati Bell, General Motors, and American Express, respectively.

So, the stakes are high and there is a lot to be learned from the experiences of others. And, having it all in one place makes for a great resource for every outsourcing professional. This book

1. Is the only major work I am aware of that focuses specifically on captive centers

2. Positions captive centers within the full range of sourcing options available today

3. Analyzes in depth the strategies of the world's most successful companies

4. Details experiences of six centers, including the challenges each company faced at each stage in its evolution, how they worked through those challenges, and the results they achieved

5. Consolidates the results in a cohesive management framework for setting up and running world-class captive centers.

As a profession and industry, outsourcing has created one of the most important organizational and industry structural shifts of the past fifty years. Captive centers are an important part of this revolution and should be an essential component of every organization's management portfolio.

Michael F. Corbett
Chairman, International Association of Outsourcing Professionals

# Acknowledgments

I thank Chun Ming Liew, Anne Katrin Debusmann, Claudio Hasler, and Stephen Kronenburg, alumni of the CEMS master's degree in international management program at Rotterdam School of Management, who under my supervision greatly contributed to research on captive centers. I will always be indebted to this young, ambitious, and talented group of people.

I am grateful to Rotterdam School of Management and Erasmus Research Institute of Management for their continuous support in my research.

I thank my editor, Darcie Carsner Torres, for the work she did on the manuscript.

My gratitude also goes to the people at the MIT Press for their hard work and dedication. In particular, I thank Jane Macdonald for all the enthusiasm and professionalism that helped bring this research project to its conclusion.

Last but not least are the three most important people in my life: my wife, Julia, who spent hours on the manuscript and gave me advice, support, and endless love; and my daughter, Dari, and my baby boy, Eden, who are the joy of my life. I will never be able to thank you enough, Julia, Dari, and Eden, for everything you have given me, so I will simply say, "Thank you."

# List of Contributors

**Anne Katrin Debusmann** is a consultant at a global leading commercial and investment bank. She holds the CEMS master's degree in international management from Rotterdam School of Management, the Netherlands. Her final project focused on captive centers in India. She made contributions in this book for the following cases: GlobalAirline, ConsumerGoods, GlobalSoftware, ITConsulting (shared captive), and AmeriBank.

**Claudio Hasler** is an industry analyst at Google, Switzerland. He holds the CEMS master's degree in international management from the Rotterdam School of Management, the Netherlands. His final project focused on the migration of captive centers. His contribution in this book is in the area of captive migration, in particular, the ITConsulting case in chapter 10.

**Julia Kotlarsky** is associate professor at Warwick Business School, Coventry, U.K. She holds a Ph.D. from Rotterdam School of Management, the Netherlands. She has published numerous journal articles and books on the topic of globally distributed team and outsourcing. Her contribution to this book is in the area of country attractiveness.

**Stephen Kronenburg**  is a consultant at Kirkman Company, the Netherlands. He holds the CEMS master's degree in international business from Rotterdam School of Management, the Netherlands. His final project focused on the expansion of captive centers. His contribution to this book is in the area of captive center trends in Global Fortune 250 firms.

**Chun-Ming Liew**  is an entrepreneur who started Direct HR, a China-focused recruitment firm specializing in the recruitment of multilingual professionals with a technical background. He holds the CEMS master's degree in international management from Rotterdam School of Management, the Netherlands. His final project focused on understanding trends in captive centers in India. His contribution to this book is in the area of trends in captive centers.

**Leslie P. Willcocks**  is professor of technology, work and globalization at the London School of Economics and Political Science. He is considered an authority in the area of outsourcing. His contribution to this book is in the area of country attractiveness.

# Synopsis

Captive centers are wholly owned subsidiaries that provide services, such as IT and back office activities, to the parent firm. However, recent evidence from the Fortune Global 250, as reported in this book, illustrates a different reality. Some captive centers have outsourced some of their activities to a local vendor, and others have expanded by providing services to external clients. Divesting the captive center is another option that some parent companies have considered, and in other cases, the captive center has been closed.

These strategic moves bring to the fore two main challenges. First, how should a parent company strategically perceive its captive center in view of its allocation and utilization of resources? Second, what sets of capabilities should be developed offshore to support the evolution of a captive center?

By examining the strategies pursued by Fortune Global 250 firms, this book shows how the basic concept of the captive center has evolved, and explores the strategic path available to managers who are considering setting up a captive center in an offshore location in order to maximize the capabilities and advantages they offer.

# 1 The Emergence of Captive Centers: Why Captive Centers, and Why Now?

Throughout the past few decades, large multinational companies such as General Electric, Texas Instruments, and Motorola have established captive centers in various foreign countries, most notably India. Captive centers are wholly owned subsidiaries that provide services, in the form of back office activities, to the parent company from an offshore location. While traditionally they have kept most of their offshore tasks in-house, numerous information technology service providers that have emerged within the Indian marketplace have developed the capabilities to execute both simple and complex work projects—a few of the most recognizable companies being Tata Consultancy Services, Infosys, and Wipro. These companies can often provide services at a lower cost than their Western competitors.

This development has enabled Western multinationals to consider alternatives in the way they implement their offshoring strategies (as depicted in figure 1.1). As just one example, in 2006, SAP Hosting Services in Bangalore outsourced several of its services to Tata Consultancy Services, also based in Bangalore. Many other companies have pursued an approach in which certain specific, often noncore, activities have been outsourced to local service providers, while

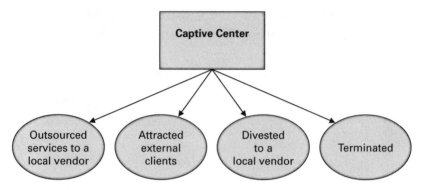

**Figure 1.1**
Alternative implementations of offshoring strategies

core activities remain in-house (i.e., in a captive center). Other companies, such as Standard Chartered and Hewlett Packard, have followed a different approach in which their captive centers provide services to both the parent company and external clients.

Other companies seem to have outgrown their offshore captive strategies. British Airways, for example, sold a majority stake of its captive center to a private equity firm, Warburg Pincus, in 2002. Apple went even further and shut down its development center in India in 2006.

Indeed, the worldwide economic crisis beginning in 2008 has raised many questions about the continuing viability of captive center models in sourcing. The worldwide drop in demand for goods and services has significantly affected companies in all industries. Questions of efficacy have surfaced as major Fortune 250 companies divested their captive endeavors throughout late 2008 and 2009. In October 2008, Citi divested its business process outsourcing (BPO) center in India to TCS, and in May 2009, it sold its Indian information technology (IT) center to Wipro.[1] Similarly, AXA sold its 600-person center to Capita Group in May 2009. Dell has also been a major contributor to the sell-off phenomenon. In October 2008, it sold its El Salvador support center to Stream Global Services[2;] in March 2009, it sold its Pasay consumer tech support center to Teleperformance[3;] and in July 2009, it sold its refurbishing plant in Lebanon to Genco Supply Chain Solutions.[4]

And this is just the tip of the iceberg. The year 2009 saw sales of captive centers in India by American Express, UBS, and AIG as well.[5] Indeed, some commentators predict that captive centers are no longer needed. David Rutchik of Pace Harmon, an outsourcing consultancy, believes that captive centers have become a drain on many companies:[6] "The larger issue is that these captive centers are difficult to manage and quite a distraction from a company's core business. They haven't been the panacea they were expected to be." Rutchik cites several reasons for this. First, captive centers represent a large, fixed cost for companies. In times of recession, getting these captive centers off the books and gaining some much-needed capital from the sales offers a short-term benefit. Second, as Indian and other outsourcing providers have improved their capabilities over the last few years, Rutchik thinks that captive centers may no longer seem worth the effort: "It takes a lot of overhead and management attention to manage internal facilities. . . . You're exposing yourself to a lot of administrative burden just to do back-office type work in lower-cost locations."

However, in spite of these and other divestitures, the captive center model, according to the latest data by Everest Research Institute, has not collapsed.[7] As of the fourth quarter of 2009, captive projects were in fact beginning to rebound. Everest reports that in the third quarter, there were twenty-eight captive announcements compared to forty in the fourth quarter, a twenty-four-month high. Salil Dani, senior research analyst for Everest, states that although there were many divestitures of captive centers in 2009, more new captives were established than there were divestitures: twenty to thirty new captives announced per quarter compared to three to four divestitures. Dani cites risk and sensitivity preferences and regulatory considerations as main drivers of the captive model.

Everest Research also revealed other significant trends in both captive and third-party outsourcing models. India and the Philippines continue to account for 40 to 45 percent of new delivery centers for both captive and third-party entities.[8] There were thirty-five new captive announcements and a marked increase in offshore activity in Brazil, China, India, and the Philippines, with forty-four new delivery centers.[9] Asian tier I cities, which are the most attractive cities for offshoring such as Bangalore and Mumbai in India, are reporting increased activity compared to tier II cities (e.g., Pune and Kolkata).

These developments bring to the fore significant challenges. First, how should a parent company strategically perceive its captive center in view of its allocation and use of resources? Second, what sets of capabilities should companies develop offshore to support the evolution of a captive center?

By examining the strategies pursued by the Fortune Global 250, this book demonstrates how the basic concept of the captive center has evolved. We present the various strategic pathways available to managers who are considering setting up a captive center in an offshore location and want to maximize its capabilities and the advantages that captive centers offer.

We also examine recent trends involving offshore captive centers. We analyze the strategies that Fortune 250 firms have pursued as they set up their first captive centers and then track the changes in those strategies in the longer term as these multinationals used their offshore captive center strategies to meet different business needs. Research shows that between 1990 and 2009, Global Fortune 250 companies established 367 captive centers worldwide. These 367 captive centers were owned by 137 companies (54.8 percent). Furthermore, 77 of these companies own more than one captive center. Thirty percent of these captive centers have changed their strategy over time, mainly from providing services to the parent firm to servicing external clients, outsourcing to local vendors, or in some cases, being divested, moved, or terminated.

We argue that offshore captive center strategies tend to evolve based on the strategic intent of the parent company and conditions in the destination country. Therefore, offshore captive centers will gain momentum only as multinationals seek to reap the value of their initial investment in an offshore operation (and in some cases, minimize losses). But what captive center strategies should multinationals pursue, and what is the evolutionary path they should follow? This chapter offers a brief summary of our findings. The final chapter of this book describes in detail both captive center strategies and capabilities.

**The Fundamental Framework of Captive Center Strategies**

We have identified six fundamental types of captive centers (see figure 1.2). The basic captive center focuses on providing services to the parent firm only, the shared captive center

services external clients as well, the hybrid option refers to
the case when a captive center outsources an offshored operation to a local vendor, the divested option encompasses the
sale of part or all of the captive center by the parent firm, the
migrated captive center suggests the relocation of the business unit to another location, and the terminated captive
center represents the case in which the captive center was
closed down. .

Our research shows that the basic captive center has
evolved into a hybrid, shared, or divested model. In our data
set, we identified three evolutionary paths: basic-shared-
divested, basic-hybrid, and basic-divested; however, one can
envisage nearly any evolutionary path depicted in figure
1.2. In some cases, the captive center will initiate its own

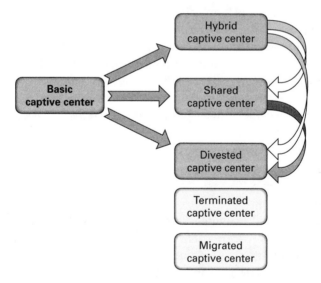

**Figure 1.2**
The six fundamental types of captive centers

evolutionary development (basic-hybrid); in other cases, especially those involving ownership changes, the parent firm will decide which path the captive unit will follow (basic-divest or basic-shared-divest). We describe the full range of captive center strategies in chapters 3 and 11. The terminated captive center and the migrated captive center do not offer an evolutionary path. These models and their implications are discussed in detail in chapters 10 and 11.

## A Historical Perspective on Offshoring and Captive Centers

Offshoring has emerged as a major trend in international business. Over the past decade, the issue of whether to offshore business processes has become one of the most vigorously debated topics in management. Decisions concerning offshoring are rooted in much larger strategic business concerns. Generally companies consider offshoring when they face decreasing profit margins stemming from competitive pressures[10] or are interested in accelerating their value chain activities. Considering this choice is a strategic reaction for companies confronting rising costs and fiercer competition.[11]

The roots of offshoring lie in the mercantilism and imperialism of the seventeenth century. The East India Company first established its own factories in India, recognizing the cost-effectiveness, flexibility, and viability of having a company foothold in the targeted trade country. The idea of establishing company-owned factories in host countries quickly swept commercial trade endeavors and expanded to such industries as sugar and rum processing and trade. Thus, the concept of offshoring has been around for centuries. In the modern day, this has become more visible since U.S. multinationals began to offshore labor-intensive manufacturing processes to low-cost developing countries such as Mexico and Panama.

One significant new development within the concept of offshoring began in the mid-1990s. Companies such as Citicorp and American Express set up offshore facilities to carry out enterprise-wide activities, such as converting data from one medium to another (e.g., converting paper documents to digital data in corporate databases).[12] Since then, significant technological developments, such as telecom bandwidth, satellite technology, and the Internet, have eliminated distance issues, enabling information to be sent around the world in seconds at marginal costs. Overall, a high degree of global collaboration has been evident since these developments in the 1990s.

In *The World Is Flat*, Thomas Friedman describes how a Web-enabled global playing field has been created as a result of the convergence of ten flattening factors, among them the introduction of search engines and work flow applications and the growing tendency to outsource and offshore work.[13] These factors offer a real-time platform for collaboration and knowledge sharing to almost anyone on the globe. Following these developments, information technology requirements such as software maintenance and development could be carried out at lower cost in countries such as Israel, Singapore, India, the Philippines, and China.[14]

In the late 1990s, numerous companies worldwide anticipated major IT problems at the turn of the millennium, dubbed the Y2K problems, for which significant numbers of programmers were required. Reliable, trained programmers were unavailable in local markets such as the United States in the numbers required to address the potential issues the new millennium presented. India had the resources available to adjust software to correct potential Y2K problems envisioned by the business community. One issue arose concerning the quality of the IT services provided in India: Would Indian companies compare to the expertise offered by programmers and software companies in the home country? The Center for eBusiness at MIT found that projects developed in India only had 10 percent more bugs than comparable projects in the United States.[15] Furthermore, Indian software development teams quickly began using quality assurance programs such as Six Sigma and Capability Maturity Model Integration (CMMI) approaches to quality management issues, which made their processes more reliable and equivalent to those of Western software development teams.[16] Although this fact had become apparent to several businesses, more and more companies witnessed the high quality of IT services that Indian companies offered, and soon other activities such as call centers, accounting services, payroll administration, debt collection, and even clinical research were transferred offshore to India.[17] Although most of the jobs transferred offshore were considered dead-end types of jobs in countries such as the United States, they offered relatively high pay to the offshore communities and were viewed with respect.

When companies consider the strategies available with respect to offshore work, they basically look at two options. One is to offshore the desired activities and processes while still maintaining them in-house through the captive center: wholly owned facilities with the purpose of processing activities that were previously done in a company's back office in the domestic country. Alternatively, they can outsource the activities and processes to an external service provider located offshore. Most companies initiate the process of offshoring by choosing one of these two options. Companies have steadily increased the volume of work outsourced to external service providers located offshore, and a large number have also set up captive centers in offshore locations to maintain internal control of the business process. The number of captive centers has steadily grown over the past few decades.

Most captive centers are set up for one or more of the following three major reasons: to reduce costs, access skilled and qualified personnel, or expand and enter new markets.[18] Indeed, captive centers have delivered value through cost savings, increased productivity and quality, and innovation. One highly visible example of successful captive center offshoring activity is demonstrated by Dell's Indian captive center, which developed process innovations that were later diffused worldwide to other Dell factories.[19]

Some companies began their offshoring experience pursuing both options. For many large multinationals, offshoring some specific operations was seen as an ordinary development, as the CEO of Siemens explained: "Offshoring is a funny thing for an international company. Where is your shore? My shore is as much in India and China as it is in Germany or the US."[20]

Multinationals have set up captive centers in various countries and regions, including India, China, Central Europe, and Latin America. India has nevertheless become the dominant location for captive centers in the world. Since the beginning of this century, the number of captive centers in India has grown rapidly: Among the Forbes 2000 companies, 44 had captive centers in India in 2000, 71 in 2003, and 110 in 2006.[21] Everest Research Group found that large North American and European firms offshored about $9 billion worth of IT and business process outsourcing work to captive center facilities in India in 2006.[22]

Among the most important factors affecting companies in their decision to set up captive centers in India are the country's vast human capital, the sophisticated level of education, and the relatively low language barrier.[23] Indeed, the Indian captive market employs over 200,000 employees and accounts for 30 percent of the Indian offshore services market.

The economies of offshoring are clear. A programmer in the United States, for example, earns around $100,000 a year in comparison to a programmer with the same qualifications and skills in India, who earns $30,000 or less (2008 figures). Farrell found that U.S. companies saved a significant amount of money when offshoring to India.[24] She states that American companies save fifty-eight cents on every dollar spent on jobs moved to India, with the main saving coming from the significant disparity in wages. Additional savings stem from bundling activities in one location, which results in a gain from economies of scale. Moreover the shortage of qualified labor in the Western world is another main driver of the increasing number of companies that offshore business and other IT-related processes.[25]

The technology boom in the 1990s, coupled with the Y2K effect on computer systems, resulted in a significant increase in programmer wages in Western countries. This strained budgets and forced companies to search for alternatives abroad in India, China, and countries in eastern Europe.[26] Technological advancement and availability has been one of the main drivers of service offshoring worldwide. These technological developments made the dispersal of business activities across the globe over the last decade possible. The rapid development in telecommunications and related areas, such as the Internet, is another facilitating factor. Figure 1.3 presents an overview of the top four drivers for offshoring software, product development, and other

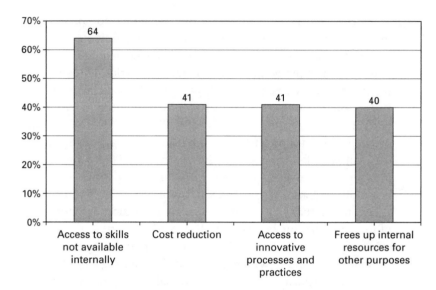

**Figure 1.3**
Top drivers of offshoring (Oshri and Kotlarsky 2009)

business functions: access to skills not available locally, cost reduction, access to innovative processes and practices, and freeing up of internal resources for other purposes. This figure presents the outcomes of a pan-European survey that I carried out with Julia Kotlarsky in 2009. The sample consisted of 263 of the largest European firms that "do," "do not," or "are considering" offshoring.

According to the research findings, access to skills is the most important motivator affecting the decision to offshore IT and business processes, followed by costs saving as the second driver. The results of our survey represent the shift in executives' mind-set regarding offshoring. It is about accessing skills and expertise not available in-house rather than only achieving reductions on the IT cost base.

Offshoring is also about opportunities and not just exploitation. However, we acknowledge that in some business processes, cutting costs will continue to be the main driver, such as with call center operations. Research also suggests that a large percentage of businesses that are currently offshoring certain activities are also planning new projects abroad in the near future (figure 1.4).[27] Call center activities are one of the projects frequently cited as an area for new implementation. This phenomenon is surprising because of growing evidence that some large firms, even those from the Fortune Global list, have closed their captive call centers because of customer dissatisfaction.[28] Many of these companies have already moved their call center operations back to their home country.

Setting up a captive unit in an offshore location is not free of challenges and involves more than simply hiring

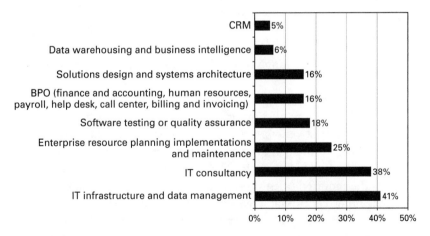

**Figure 1.4**
Future project plans for offshoring companies (Oshri and Kotlarsky 2009)

employees, renting a building, and installing hardware. Considering the competitive nature of the offshoring market and high employee turnover, a significant investment is required to obtain high-quality human resource professionals and processes, software development process optimization, state-of-the-art training facilities, engagement management expertise, and service management expertise.

Many other challenges arise through the adoption and implementation of captive centers. For example, some firms have struggled with ever increasing costs, employee attrition, and the lack of integration and management support.[29] Some experts suggest that the nature and purpose of captive centers must evolve to be successful; for example WNS, previously owned by British Airways, has evolved from a basic captive providing services to a parent firm to a larger center that now provides services to international customers as well. Small-sized captive centers are often hard to maintain because they offer little long-term career growth to employees, resulting in a high level of attrition. Such negative impacts on captive centers have led firms to explore a wider range of strategic options that are available offshore.

One area that requires more in-depth exploration is the question of why offshoring and outsourcing work for some firms but not others. The problem stems from the widely held view that offshoring is a universally applicable solution for reducing costs, creating flexibility, and broadening access to the required talent pool that is not currently available in the home country at a reasonable cost.[30] Contrary to popular belief, offshoring is not a single strategic model applicable to every business need, intention, or process. Rather, it comprises a variety of models, each with its own risks and benefits to consider and address. Successful offshoring depends heavily on choosing the appropriate model to fit the specified business need as much as it does on a cost–benefit analysis of performing the same activities at home.

## The Present and Future of Captive Centers

Today firms have allocated about $1.7 trillion to manage and process back office operations. With an annual growth of about 5 percent in outsourcing and offshoring and the emergence of new offshoring locations (estimated at about 120 countries around the globe) that are offering IT and business processes services, captive centers will continue to play a role in sourcing arrangements. We have identified seven trends for the present and future of captive centers.

1. More captive centers will be built by large firms looking to reduce costs and access skills that are not available in-house.

2. Central and eastern Europe will emerge as the most attractive location for European multinationals to set up captive centers in the next five years. Nearshoring, which is the sourcing of IT and business services to a relatively close country, will also be a strong trend in captive centers for North American multinationals.

3. Captive centers will continue to be sold for two main reasons: many captive centers (at the moment about 60 percent) will struggle to become or remain successful and therefore will drive their parent firms to look for a buyer. Captive centers that have built large scale or developed an area of specialization complementary to the commonly found expertise in the local vendor market will become attractive for an investment house or a local vendor and therefore will eventually be divested.

4. Large captive centers in maturing and mature outsourcing markets such as India will expand outsourcing offshore activities to local vendors in an effort to transform the captive center from a service and cost center into a profit and innovation center and free up talent to focus on value-adding activities.

5. Small- and medium-sized enterprises will explore ways to use existing captive center facilities as pools of expertise in order to reduce costs as well as access skills at a global level. This will accelerate the evolution of captive centers into the shared captive center model.

6. Many multinationals with captive centers will struggle to sell their offshore assets. These are mainly captive centers that failed to build up scale or develop a unique area of expertise that is complementary to the mainstream line of expertise commonly found in the local vendor market.

7. The captive center concept will move from the experimentation stage to the maturity stage, significantly reducing the number of captive center terminations.

**Key Terms and Definitions**

This section sets out the common terms and definitions used throughout this book:

*Back office functions*   The tasks dedicated to running the company such as those involved in developing the products or involved in administration but without being seen by customers. Although the operations of a back office are usually not given much consideration, they are a major contributor to business organization and process. This is in contrast to front office functions such as sales.

*Basic captive center*   A wholly owned branch office or subsidiary, used mainly for IT support, back office data processing, call center operations, software development, or business process outsourcing in an offshore location. These services are provided only to the parent firm.

*Business process outsourcing (BPO)*   The transfer of either entire or portions of business processes to a third-party service provider—for example, accounting, human resources, and procurement. Companies that are considering BPO options can choose from three options: a strategic alliance, a joint venture, and offshore outsourcing. Business processes can also be provided from an offshore captive center.

*Build-operate-transfer (BOT) model*   A model in which a client contracts with an offshore or nearshore vendor to execute an outsourcing arrangement whereby the vendor will build and operate the service center (e.g., call center or any other business process) for an extended period of time. The client retains the right to take over the operation under certain conditions and certain financial arrangements.

*Divestiture of captive center*   The sale of a captive unit, in whole or in part.

*Hybrid captive center*   A captive center that outsources some of its own offshored processes to external service providers.

*Joint venture in the outsourcing or offshoring context*   A partnership between a client firm and an offshore vendor whereby the parties contribute resources to the new venture. Many of the offshoring joint ventures  have a BOT component built into the agreement.

*Migrated captive center*   A captive center whose operations have relocated to another offshore location, terminating the functions in the original location.

*Offshoring*   The practice of moving the business operations and processes of a company to a location based outside the home country by contracting with an offshore service provider (offshore outsourcing) or through a captive center model (offshore captive center). Offshoring can also be defined as moving operations beyond the home continent, whereas nearshoring is referenced when a company maintains business operations close to the home country (same continent).

*Outsourcing*   Contracting with a third-party service provider for the completion of a certain amount of work, for a specified length of time, cost, and level of service.

*Shared captive center*   A captive center that performs work for both the parent company and external third-party clients.

*Shared service center*   An operational approach of centralizing administrative and business processes that were once carried out in separate divisions or locations—for example, finance, procurement, human resources, and IT. A shared service center can be a captive center, but not necessarily a shared captive center.

**The Structure of This Book**

This book is divided into two parts: "The Fundamentals of Captive Centers" and "Captive Centers in Practice" (see figure 1.5).

**Part I: The Fundamentals of Captive Centers**
Chapter 2 analyzes the various types of outsourcing and offshoring models available. It discusses how each method works, the advantages and disadvantages of each model,

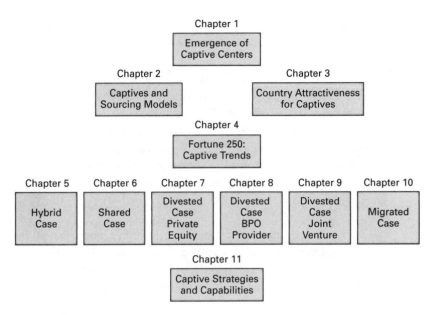

**Figure 1.5**
The structure of this book

and the capabilities and motives behind the decision to implement a specific model. The chapter introduces a basic guideline for analyzing whether to outsource specific tasks and processes within the business organization. It also defines the different types of captive centers: basic, hybrid, shared, migrated, divested, and terminated.

Chapter 3 discusses the factors affecting country attractiveness for captive centers. This chapter provides a practical guide for country selection through numerous examples of BRIC (Brazil, Russia, India, and China) and non-BRIC countries.

Chapter 4 analyzes recent captive trends emerging among Fortune Global 250 companies in order to provide the backdrop and foundation for the case study research and findings presented in part II of this book.

## Part II: Captive Centers in Practice

Part II focuses on detailed case studies of the captive models: basic, hybrid, shared, divested, and migrated.

Chapter 5 examines the GlobalSoftware case, wherein the parent company's basic captive unit evolved into a complex hybrid structure to address the growing needs of the parent company. We examine the challenges faced, the solutions implemented, and the capabilities developed through the evolutionary journey.

Chapter 6 examines the case of ITConsulting, a basic Hungarian captive center that evolved into a shared service center that contributed value to the parent company by offering its capabilities and services to third-party international customers.

Chapter 7 examines the case of GlobalAirline and its captive unit, GlobalOutsourcer, established in 1996. GlobalAirline first developed its basic captive center into a shared structure, which allowed the center to develop critical expertise and expand its domain knowledge through a variety of external clients. However, in order to expand the unit's capabilities, GlobalAirline divested most of its stake in GlobalOutsourcer to a private equity firm because it was not willing to devote the necessary resources to expanding the company to its full potential.

Chapter 8 examines the case of AmeriBank, one of the world's largest financial services banks, which set up a basic captive center through a strategic buyout in 1992. In 1999 the captive was restructured into a publicly traded BPO provider responsible for corporate and consumer banking. In October 2008 AmeriBank divested its captive unit through a BPO provider buyout to IndiaIT, a leading Indian BPO company.

Chapter 9 examines the case of ConsumerGoods, which established an independently run Indian BPO unit offering finance and accounting back office services. ConsumerGoods divested the captive entity to Consulting& Outsourcing through a joint venture agreement in order to externalize and develop its customer base. The divestiture allowed Consulting&Outsourcing to broaden its global service offerings, incorporating financial and IT services under one umbrella.

Chapter 10 examines the case of InfoTech, a global provider of IT services. InfoTech represents a case of captive center migration, in which low-value functions performed in its captive unit in Budapest were migrated to a new center in Sofia, where costs were lower. This enabled the Budapest center to take on higher-value functions from the regional units and move up the company value chain.

Chapter 11 summarizes the findings of the case studies presented in chapters 5 through 10 and sets out some general implications for captive center capabilities and strategies moving forward into the future.

# I   The Fundamentals of Captive Centers

# 2  Captive Center and Other Sourcing Models

Understanding captive centers as a sourcing business model should start by positioning this concept within the sourcing literature. Much has been written and said in recent years about sourcing, and the academic and business jargon has expanded to include such new terms as *right-shoring, best-shoring, nearshoring,* and many more. Nevertheless, the key sourcing models, such as outsourcing, offshore outsourcing, and offshoring (e.g., captive models), remain the most prominent sourcing vehicles. In the end, much of the sourcing discourse has focused on understanding the risks and mitigating strategies and capabilities for either outsourcing or offshore outsourcing.

Since the end of the twentieth century, another option regarding the make-versus-buy dilemma has arisen: the development of captive centers. Between 1995 and 2000, more than 80 out of 250 researched companies had set up captive centers in India.[1] The captive center model has become well established, with hundreds of these centers set up and operating around the globe.

Over the past several years, captive centers have evolved, and newly generated strategies have been devised.[2] These development paths include the hybrid, shared, and divested captive center, briefly described in chapter 1. According to Levina, a company should consider captive centers as a viable alternative in the offshoring process when discussing outsourcing business processes and back office functions.[3] A decision between offshore outsourcing and setting up a captive center should be based on the scale and scope of human capital and operational capabilities. During the evaluation of offshoring options, joint ventures are often set up as a compromise between outsourcing and establishing captive centers. Hybrid joint venture models most frequently evolve from wholly owned captive centers.[4]

In order to have a better understanding of the underlying strategies and development in a company's make-versus-buy decision with special attention given to the setup and evolution of captive centers, we will examine the alternative sourcing models of onshore outsourcing, offshoring, offshore outsourcing, joint ventures, and the captive center model.

## Onshore Outsourcing

Onshore outsourcing is an arrangement where a local external vendor provides services and goods to a client firm. From the client viewpoint, there are several reasons for choosing to outsource locally—in other words, domestic outsourcing. The primary reasons are proximity to the vendor, cultural fit,and familiarity with work regulations, methodologies, and values. In addition, client firms also assume they will benefit from some cost reduction, improved agility, a freeing up of talent to focus on high-value activities, and access to skills.[5] Outsourcing a business function, whether locally or offshore, often allows the client firm to reengineer the outsourced business function, improve efficiency across the value chain, and contribute to the firm's procurement capabilities.[6] According to Peter Bendor-Samuel of Everest Group, these improvements take three different forms.[7] First, the quality of the service itself may be intrinsically improved through better accuracy or service time, for example. Second, the business may achieve a greater impact through higher customer satisfaction and increased efficiency. Third, the strategic impact will be realized through cycle time gains or competitive positioning.

Until the late 1990s, onshore outsourcing mainly held an advantage over offshoring because it provided access to innovations and new ideas, while offshoring focused on cheap labor markets.[8] However, this advantage has become less marked in recent years as innovation and new ideas are now generated from offshore markets as well. The major disadvantage of outsourcing as a whole lies in the inherent loss of control over outsourced business processes. In addition, outsourcing costs may increase if the client firm is not ready for outsourcing.

Although onshore outsourcing has some similarities to offshoring and offshore outsourcing, the key aspects in managing onshore outsourcing are different. First, onshore outsourcing projects do not face language and culture differences or any issues relating to distance. Nevertheless, client firms engaged in onshore outsourcing still need to pay attention to critical processes such as vendor selection and contract management.

## Offshoring

For the purposes of this book, *offshoring* is the movement of business operations and processes to any location based outside the home country, which is usually on a different continent. Offshoring can be carried out through the use of a third-party service provider located in an offshore country (offshore outsourcing) or by setting up a wholly owned subsidiary in an offshore location (offshore captive center).

Offshoring IT and business processes began in the late 1980s when businesses began outsourcing to cheaper labor markets, mainly in the health care industry, the telecom industry, and the technology sector.[9] Offshoring became a popular choice because of the availability of low-cost skilled labor in offshore locations that was able to provide services through powerful electronic platforms. For example, in the late 1980s and early 1990s, demand for cheap, low-level data-entry personnel who had mastered the English language led to a surge in offshoring to India and the Philippines.[10] Subsequently, during the tech boom that started in the mid-1990s, offshoring was mainly considered as a means of hiring cheap software developers and programmers of relatively comparable quality as those in the home country.[11] Offshore projects today are motivated by a demand for innovative, technologically advanced, low-cost personnel.

**Offshore Outsourcing**

Offshore outsourcing has grown rapidly since the 1990s. Firms have disaggregated their supply and value chains to capitalize on the availability of low-cost, highly skilled experts in offshore locations. As companies acquired more experience with offshoring, offshore outsourcing has come to be seen by client firms as an extension of the onshore outsourcing strategy, though with some specific challenges that require the deployment of additional resources and solutions. Offshore outsourcing was also promoted by governments seeking to increase foreign direct investment and the growth of their local service sector. India, for example, offered unique tax benefits for multinationals that invested in offshoring.

Three main strategic approaches are used for offshore outsourcing: a short-term tactical approach, a strategic, long-term horizon approach, and a transformational approach, that is, changing the entire business model of the client firm.[12] The underlying reasons for each approach are outlined in table 2.1.

Offshore outsourcing offers much deeper cost savings than onshore outsourcing, though the risks are also high.[13] In essence, offshore outsourcing raises some of the same concerns as onshore outsourcing. However, some additional challenges are associated with offshore outsourcing, such as cultural idiosyncrasies, language barriers, and time zone differences. There can be a sense of losing control of the outsourced business process because of the distance and

**Table 2.1**
The three main approaches to offshore outsourcing

| Tactical | Strategic | Transformational |
|---|---|---|
| Reduces and controls operating expenses | Improves business focus | Brings new and faster solutions |
| Provides free investment | Gives access to world-class capabilities | Shortens product life cycles |
| Provides cash infusion | Accelerates re-engineering efforts | Redefines relationships with suppliers and others |
| Makes internal resources available | Shares risks | Offers entry to new markets |
| Functions are difficult to manage internally | Frees resources for other purposes | Develops new/flexible business models |

different work and legal mentalities involved. For example, in some countries, the notion of intellectual property rights is understood and applied completely differently than in most Western countries.[14] Fear of losing knowledge, unclear return on investment, and unmet expectations are considered some of the drawbacks in offshore outsourcing, and distance especially is an obstacle to quickly fixing troubled offshore outsourcing projects.[15] Nonetheless, offshore outsourcing has been widely exercised by Western firms, and the experience gained since the late 1990s has certainly improved the way most firms now address these challenges.

**Joint Ventures**

With the increasing interest by client firms in exploiting off-shoring opportunities, joint ventures have been increasingly applied since the 1990s. A joint venture is basically a partner-ship between a client firm and an offshore vendor. In this arrangement, the offshore partner provides expertise to the joint venture unit. The new venture engages in providing offshore outsourcing services to the client firm and also insourcing services to the joint venture in the form of skills and capabilities.

Joint ventures are set up largely to decrease the high risk posed by both offshore outsourcing and captive center models. They are particularly relevant for client firms that seek to invest in a development capability offshore. These firms initially do not have assets in the offshore country necessary to build a development center and do not see an immediate need to invest in building offshore assets; however, offshore outsourcing is also not appealing to them because of the high risk, the lack of sourcing management capabilities, and a desire to maintain some control over the outsourced process.[16] Quartz, for example, is an integrated package and banking platform for the international financial industry. It was developed jointly by Tata Consultancy Services (TCS) and Teknosoft (TKS), a Swiss-based company that specializes in financial services, through a partnership in which the technical knowledge and experience of TCS in providing computing services was combined with the business knowledge of TKS of the financial industry and banking. The advantages offered through the joint ventures model are similar to those offered by offshore outsourcing; however, under this arrangement, the vendor and client firm engage in much more intense learning and knowledge sharing, which offers higher value for both sides.[17] Furthermore, the joint venture model allows client firms to reduce the risk in offshoring while benefiting from the higher control over outsourced processes and access to lower-cost talent pools.

Disadvantages of this model are the large penalties that can be incurred by noncontractual termination. The business must take into account that until the point of transfer, all resources are still owned by the build-operate-transfer (BOT) models partner. Although the company gains more control over outsourced processes, one partner can play off another and take unfair advantage of this collaboration–a problem that does not arise with the captive center option.[18]

## Captive Centers

Managers in offshoring projects often make the mistake of "assuming that migrating operations offshore requires *outsourcing* them to another company," says Simeon Preston, senior manager with Marakon Associates.[19] However,

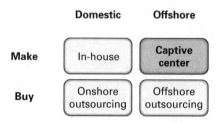

**Figure 2.1**
Captive centers in the make-buy matrix

offshoring does not necessarily mean outsourcing (buying a product or service from an external vendor); it can also stand for in-house offshoring (producing a product or service by internal processes located outside the home country) by setting up a wholly owned subsidiary overseas, known as a captive center (figure 2.1).

Captive centers emerged at the end of the twentieth century and became more visible in the twenty-first century. In 1997, General Electric Capital International Services became one of the first companies to open a captive center in India.[20] While pioneer firms mainly set up information technology (IT) captive centers, both business process outsourcing (BPO) and IT captive centers are now primary areas for development.[21] Over 500 captive centers have been set up in India,[22] of which 70 percent are wholly owned subsidiaries.[23] The captive center market is expected to see an annual growth of 30 percent,[24] and Infosys anticipates that some existing captive centers will increase their headcount by 50 percent per annum.[25]

To gain an understanding with respect to the various industries that set up captive centers, the size of the market, market trends, and the geographic locations, we have studied this phenomenon intensively over the past four years. Our findings show that the main sectors that use the captive center model are banking and finance, along with computer and network. Other researchers have discovered that global businesses often enter the market with one captive center and set up other offshore in-house operations after their test centers have proven successful.[26]

Captive centers are often created in pursuit of the same financial benefits as offshore outsourcing. The total costs of captive center operations were analyzed by Soreon Research GmbH. According to Fran Karamouzis, research vice president at Gartner Research and Advisory Services in Stamford, Connecticut, companies setting up captive centers were able to save 30 to 70 percent in costs over five to seven years.[27] Companies also see not having to share assets, intellectual property rights, or core competencies as important reasons to set up captive centers. This is particularly true of businesses that have little experience in outsourcing and need to retain higher levels of control over core activities in order to reduce the risk of information and knowledge loss.[28] Setting up captive centers from scratch requires the company to use its own resources as well as local expertise, and requires a thorough understanding of the market of the offshore location.[29]

A company's decision to either outsource to a third-party provider or set up a captive center is influenced by political and regulatory changes and taxation, as well as foreign investment regulations and development of the local labor markets.[30] Other factors influencing the establishment of captive centers are the availability of English-speaking staff, the scale of the workforce, and the educational systems in the host country.[31]

Because the development of captive centers has been examined only narrowly, conflicting arguments about their underlying strategies exist. Researchers such as Sudan Apte from Forrester Research state that the majority of decisions to set up captive centers are driven by personal reasons, such as being close to family and friends.[32] Oshri, Kotlarsky, and Liew see the genesis of captive centers as arising out of the insufficient infrastructure of offshore locations, which is why wholly owned subsidiaries with the necessary knowledge, resources, and communication structure must be set up.[33] According to Ghosh and Iyer, the decision to offshore in-house stems from the absence of credible third-party off-shore providers with adequate resources during the first phase of setting up captive centers.[34] Furthermore, Aron points out, business process outsourcing began with larger corporations setting up captive service centers that executed enterprise-wide operations to create the necessary infrastructure in-house.[35] However, research based on more recently developed captive centers reveals that the creation of these centers in the current environment is mainly determined by the developed market of outsourcing and offshoring.[36] According to Preston, "Today, the delivery risks have become better understood, the local skills base has broadened and the communication infrastructure is robust."

In order to make the best offshore decision, a company should follow a four-step process:

1. Identify which processes and activities to offshore.

2. Determine the range of options and possibilities.

3. Value each option against strategic, financial, and organizational criteria.

4. Choose the preferred model.

These ground rules apply to the decision regarding the captive center model as well.

Once the decision is made in favor of establishing a captive center, its success depends on numerous factors: the alignment and engagement of the parent company, committed financial capital, the infrastructure and technology to establish and develop the offshore unit, automation and process efficiencies, the migration of operational practices while focusing on service quality, the international career opportunities of its staff and staff training, and the enhancement of management skills on operational risk and business continuity challenges.[37] Captive centers follow a four-phase life cycle consisting of start-up, value addition, competence accumulation, and third-party service stages.[38]

Although successful and efficient captive centers can demonstrate up to a 70 percent cost savings, about half of all captive centers fail to succeed[39] and 60 percent have trouble offering substantial and measurable benefits to the parent company.[40] Most captive centers face difficulties in the areas of product engineering, R&D, IT, and other BPO services.[41] They can appear to be less profitable than third-party providers, since they are counted as cost centers and not as profit centers set up by third-party providers, which focus more on training and asset utilization for productivity.[42] Over 60 percent of captive centers suffer from high operating costs, face above-average rates of staff turnover (about 40 percent in 2008, but these figures have come down during the global financial crisis), and sharply increased wages in recent years.[43] Planned cost models are often unrealistic, and the integration of the captive unit with the parent company suffers in many cases.[44] When compared to offshore outsourcing through a third-party service provider, captive centers are assumed to be more challenging because of the pressure to acquire needed new skills, achieve a quick impact, manage high risk, address ongoing capital needs,

build economies of scale, and gain management attention.[45]
Owing to these disadvantages and the low margins realized
by captive centers, Ghosh and Iyer predict that over 400
captive centers in India will eventually evolve into
outsourcing centers through acquisition or other business
developments.

## Establishing a Captive Center

The decision as to whether to outsource certain processes or
functions to an external service provider or establish a captive
center abroad depends on many factors. One of the main
reasons to establish a captive center, as opposed to offshore
outsourcing, is the desire of the parent firm to protect its
intellectual property. Other more common motives are cost-
effectiveness, control over the offshore operations, strong
delivery processes, considerations of customer perception,
and prior experience with offshoring.[46] Captive centers can
be set up in a variety of different ways—for example, a BOT,
a joint venture, or a fully owned subsidiary (basic captive).
In many other cases, the captive center is a result of an acquisition made by the parent firm and not necessarily a business
unit that the parent firm set up from scratch.

   The decision as to whether to outsource offshore by means
of using an external service provider abroad or a captive
center is a difficult decision and one that is heavily debated
among global business communities. Scholars and industry
professionals have not yet found a definitive answer to the
dilemma as to whether to outsource or offshore. Some predict
that the captive model will disappear completely within the
coming years, while others believe that captives will continue to be a viable alternative to offshore outsourcing.[47]

This book, which supports the latter view, argues that the captive center model will evolve into multiple business concepts that exploit the principles in offshoring but also offer new opportunities to the parent firm. We discuss these aspects in the coming chapters.

## The Evolution of Captive Center Strategies

Forrester Research predicts that 10 percent of current captive units will be shut down by their parent firms, 20 percent will evolve into a hybrid strategy, and 10 percent will be divested, with services then obtained from third-party providers.[48] Our research shows that many captive centers have already pursued these tactics by evolving from the basic model into a hybrid captive center or a shared captive center. Based on our observations, we offer six types of captive centers: the basic, the hybrid, shared, divested, terminated, and migrated models. Others who have studied this topic identify additional partnership models, such as virtual captive centers,[49] which we believe can be classified under the hybrid category. These six main types are illustrated in figure 2.2.

### Basic Captive Center

A basic captive center is a wholly owned subsidiary set up and operated by the parent company. For reasons of convenience, a large number of companies start with a basic captive center after deciding to go offshore, either due to the lack of suitable local vendors or their belief that they will be better off by maintaining this activity in-house in an offshore location. In addition, even if local vendors are available, the risks posed in loss of control of outsourced processes may be perceived as too high.

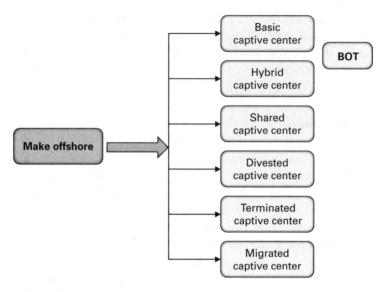

**Figure 2.2**
Main types of captive centers

### Hybrid Captive Center

Hybrid captive centers (figure 2.3) outsource parts of their own offshored processes to external, often local, vendors. They thus represent a mix between captive offshoring and offshore outsourcing. In this case, the captive center still directly provides support to the parent firm, but it also outsources some of the activities carried out offshore to a third-party service provider. The advantage of this mix is that the captive center can free up resources to focus on high-value work and reduce costs by outsourcing to a cheaper third-party vendor. The disadvantage associated with this model of captive center is the need to develop sourcing management capabilities offshore so outsourced activities are delivered at the same or better service quality by the third-party vendor.

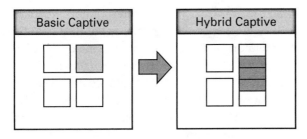

**Figure 2.3**
Hybrid captive in the make-buy matrix

Clearly the expectation is that hybrid captive centers will be considerably cheaper than basic captive centers. Bloch, Narayanan, and Seth found average cost reductions of around 30 percent using third-party vendors of financial services in India compared to maintaining fully owned subsidiaries.[50] According to Overby, third-party vendors had superior cost models due to better scale, leaner processes, lower overhead, and higher investments in knowledge transfer.[51] More specifically, captive centers were found to grant higher salaries, work fewer shifts, employ more costly expatriates, and incur higher overhead costs than the local vendors. More surprising, some reports suggested the superior quality of third-party vendors over that of captive centers, which can be credited to the high degree of vendors' specialization and their benchmarking and learning from clients through close collaboration.[52] More classical advantages of outsourcing, such as the ability to focus on the critical core issues and increased flexibility regarding production volume and staff size, were also observed.[53] Overall, hybrid captive centers combine the strength of basic captive centers (better quality and control) with the lower costs induced by third-party vendors.[54]

Many different forms of hybrid captive centers, such as virtual captive centers, exist. However, most of these can be categorized as either *joint ventures*, which outsource core activities, or *hybrids*, which outsource noncore activities.

In a joint venture, activities are outsourced to a vendor through an insourcing or outsourcing arrangement. The parent firm may turn the captive center into a joint venture model in order to increase collaboration with and learning from a local provider that offers special expertise. However, such joint ventures also run the risk that the joint venture partner does not share the same objectives as the parent firm.

**Shared Captive Centers**

Captive centers may evolve into a shared captive center unit that provides IT and business processes services to both parent firm and external clients (figure 2.4). Shared captive centers increase the volume of transactions processed offshore and therefore tend to offer better value per transaction. Consequently, successful shared captive centers become attractive for an acquisition by a local vendor.

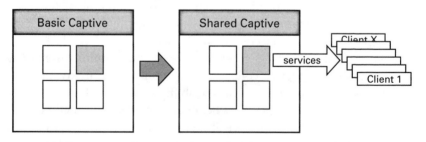

**Figure 2.4**
Shared captive center in the make-buy matrix

The shared captive center concept presents a strategy that allows the parent firm to pursue a growth strategy within its captive center. By creating a diversified clientele for the captive center, the parent firm reduces its operational risk, allows a change in its strategic direction, may increase its earnings stability, makes better use of its spare resources, and allows the captive center to learn how to adapt to customer needs. More specifically, diversifying the customer base may represent a compelling option if the captive center possesses specialized know-how valuable to external clients.[55] Additional motives for pursuing a shared captive center model are associated with the ability to improve the flexibility of personnel because employees can be relocated internally if needed and the detachment from the "one customer paradigm," which elevates the captive center's dependency on the parent firm with regard to learning and further development, that often plagues basic captive centers.[56] All of these factors can contribute to the transformation of the basic captive center from a cost center to a profit center.

Most of the captive centers that have evolved into shared captive centers have strong capabilities, such as the ability to innovate, and are therefore considered to be beneficial partners for external clients. The growth of the shared captive is fueled by investments made by the parent firm as well as the expertise provided by clients and third-party providers. Moreover, shared captive centers are often created to attract potential buyers; therefore, the extent of the investment very much depends on the parent firm's vision for the captive center's future.

### Divested Captive Center

The basic captive center can evolve into a divested captive center. Divesting a captive center means selling all or some of its operations to a buyer. Following divestment, the parent firm in most cases will become a client of the acquired captive center to ensure service continuity. Divesting captive centers can follow one of two strategies, depending on the operating mode of the buyer. The first option considers financial issues, and the second, strategic concerns.[57] In the first, captive centers are often bought because the purchasing party believes that the center value will increase over time (e.g., it may be in a high-growth area of specialization). The buying party invests in the captive center to allow further growth and segregates the center operations from other operations it might have offshore. In this way, the buying party keeps options open regarding a possible divestment for profit at later stage. In the second scenario, the buying party, often a local vendor, will seek to integrate the line of business process or IT services with its portfolio of services offshore. The goal is to improve the range of services offered by the buying party as well as to increase the scale of transactions performed offshore.

Of special interest are captive centers that first evolved into a shared captive center and subsequently were divested. In most of these cases, the basic captive centers were acquired by private equity firms with the intention of divesting the centers two to five years after acquisition, offsetting any concerns related to having a single customer base. Another divesting option is referred to as management buyouts, where the top team of the captive center buys out the captive unit of the parent firm.

These two paths to divestiture are worthy of closer examination. In the first scenario, a basic captive may be sold directly, without ever evolving into a shared structure. A popular alternative is to develop a shared captive center, which boosts its attractiveness to potential future buyers, and then divest (see figure 2.5).

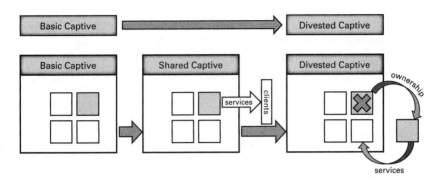

**Figure 2.5**
Modes of divested captive center

The reasons to divest a captive center are threefold. First, parent firms decide to sell because their captive center is becoming a distraction to their overall strategic objectives by drawing off management attention and requiring massive investment to support its growth path. Citigroup and Unilever, for example, decided to divest their captive centers in order to redirect their focus back to core activities and competencies.[58] Another reason is related to a captive center's poor performance. Parent firms of poorly performing captive centers will try to divest these business units as they become aware of high operational costs, pricing problems, attrition levels, rising wage costs, and increasing numbers of capable third parties.[59] Deutsche Bank, for instance, argued for divesting its captive center because it could reduce costs by outsourcing the company's IT requirements to a third-party vendor instead of maintaining these services in a captive center. In many of the cases we have studied, parent firms also make the decision to divest when they face a crisis (not necessarily relating to the captive center performance) that requires them to raise cash fast. And finally, parent firms may sell their captive center when it has reached a high maturity level in scale and quality. In this case, the captive center will attract buyers that likely will offer a significant return on the parent firm's investment.

The decision to divest a captive can be made for financial or strategic reasons. Generally divesting has had a positive impact on parent firms, buyers, and the captive center itself.

### Terminated Captive Center

In contrast to divesting, some parent firms choose not to divest or were not able to divest for various reasons, including the simple fact that buyers were not interested in the venture. Going against the general trend toward offshoring and captive centers, these parent firms decided to close down their captive centers without extracting asset value from the project (figure 2.6). When a captive center is terminated, it ceases offshore processes or is shut down.

A distinction needs to be made between captive centers that migrate operations to another country and therefore close down operations in the original location, only to reopen the doors in a different offshore (or near-shore) location, and

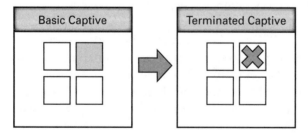

**Figure 2.6**
Path to terminating a captive center

those captive centers whose operations are transferred back to the home location. The terminated captive center is about the latter, while the former is explained in the next section. Clearly, terminating the captive center is viewed as a failure. No underlying growth strategy for this path exists—it is a cut-your-losses approach.

Several cases in our study reported later in this book, all operating call center captives, chose to shut down their captive center operations entirely and move operations back to their home country. These centers faced tremendous difficulties in language barriers, concerns about identity theft, and poor service quality.[60] Many of the firms that closed captive centers because of poor service quality were concerned with the deterioration of their reputation and brand name. In many of these cases, the parent firm decided to terminate the captive center and bring the service back to the home country instead of attempting to fix the problem.

### Migrated Captive Centers

Migration of a captive center can generally be defined as the movement of some business processes or IT support center from one country to another (figure 2.7). A new captive

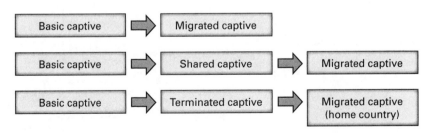

**Figure 2.7**
Possible migration paths

center will be set up while the original center ceases providing services after the assets and resources have been transferred to the new entity. In contrast to captive centers that are terminated due to a failure, migrated captive centers terminate activity in one area and relocate in accordance with an underlying strategy. Furthermore, we have observed cases in which the parent firm of a captive center has set up a new captive in a different location to specialize in the same line of business process services. We treat this strategic move as an expansion of the captive center rather than a migration strategy.

While parent firms may incur costs and challenges in transferring assets and resources to the new entity, the

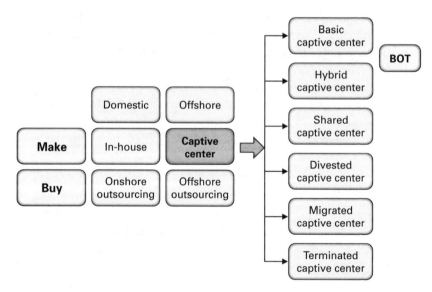

**Figure 2.8**
Make-buy matrix and the range of captive center strategies

benefits often deemed available from the migration strategy are seen to outweigh the costs.

It is not yet clear how many parent firms have migrated their captive centers, nor is it fully understood what motives lay behind such a move. However, some of the key motives that we have been able to identify include cost savings at the new location, better skills, and improved business conditions. In the end, the trend toward migration of captive centers appears to be driven by the fact that people are not looking for one country to go to, but are seeking a range of solutions or options, depending on their footprint and their customer requirements throughout the world.[61]

## Conclusion

Much of the research on offshore outsourcing has centered on defining and proving the strategies behind offshore outsourcing of business processes. However, researchers have only recently started to examine offshoring business processes in-house. Figure 2.8 shows the six setup and development paths available for captive centers, four of which have underlying strategies (the top four).

# 3    Country Attractiveness for Sourcing

Deciding where to locate a captive center has never been so complex. In the 1990s, the straightforward decision was to offshore activities to India. Now, about 120 countries compete to win information technology (IT) and business process offshoring (BPO) contracts. Obviously each country offers a different set of advantages. Certain regions are perceived as centers of excellence for a particular business process service or IT support. In exploring the attractiveness of offshoring locations and considering where to set up their captive center, executives need to assess numerous factors and drivers, such as the comparative advantage of a particular location, the skills base it offers, and its growth potential.

## An Overview of Sourcing Destinations

Together with India, which in 2009 attracted some 65 percent of the Information Technology Outsourcing (ITO) and 43 percent of the BPO market,[1] Brazil, Russia, and China are in tier 1: they are considered the most attractive destinations for outsourcing for IT and business processes. This is mainly because of the scale of services and available skills and the maturity achieved with regard to sourcing activities. Vendors as well as captive centers based in these countries, especially India, tend to move up the value chain, departing from specific and repetitive tasks that are usually captured by new entrants—the tier 2 and 3 countries.

The relative attractiveness of Brazil, Russia, India, and China (BRIC) and non-BRIC countries as sourcing destinations is dynamic. Attractiveness needs to be understood in the context of long-term global sourcing trends and the current global economic climate. In this regard, Willcocks and Lacity argue that spending will continue to rise in all global sourcing markets through recessionary as well as growth periods, but spending on business process outsourcing and offshoring will overtake the spending on IT outsourcing and offshoring by 2015.[2] Business process offshoring expenditures will occur in areas such as the human resource function; procurement; back office administration; call centers; legal, finance, and accounting; customer-facing operations; and asset management. In line with this trend, a highly competitive global services market presents opportunities for countries that offer the right mix of costs, skills and reliable service.

Emerging sourcing destinations are trying to differentiate their offerings from BRIC countries and from tier 2 and 3 rivals when competing for an investment such as a captive center. For example, Egypt is promoting itself as a low-cost destination for call centers that specialize in European languages. Dubai and Singapore present their IT security systems and legal systems as an advantage with regard to the outsourcing or offshoring of high-security and business-continuity services. The Philippines, a former U.S. colony, stresses its long cultural ties with the United States and the excellent English skills of its population in order to attract English-speaking call centers. Morocco is trying to attract

French-speaking European clients to set up call centers, while Central and South American Spanish-speaking countries are hoping to establish call centers that can provide services to the Hispanic market in the United States.[3] In fact, recent studies have shown that some non-BRIC destinations have been successful in competing with BRIC by positioning their specialized skill sets in particular areas and often by offering lower costs than other potential destinations.[4]

While second- and third-tier outsourcing and offshoring destinations are improving their position, recent years have paid witness to the leadership that India continues to gain in the areas of IT and business process outsourcing services. Many global firms view India as a center of excellence in these areas, and not just a low-cost destination. Many U.S. and European business initially engaged Indian suppliers to provide technical services such as programming and platform upgrades. But as these relationships matured, Western firms assigned more challenging work to Indian suppliers, such as development and support tasks for critical business applications, and set up captive centers in India. In our research, we learned that India now wishes to assume higher-value activities, including research and development (R&D) and knowledge process outsourcing and offshoring.

However, India, and to a lesser extent China, Brazil, and Russia, are already experiencing upward pressure on wages, combined with rising, and sometimes high, attrition. A war for talent appears to be taking place among the BRIC countries, which acts to suppress the key factors that made these countries attractive destinations for outsourcing in the first place. For example, some captive centers initially located in India and China have been relocated to more attractive destinations. In fact, some major Indian suppliers (Tata Consultancy Services, for one) are setting up their own global delivery centers in China mainly because the supply of engineering skills and proficiency in English have risen dramatically in China in recent years.

To put these views into context, China invested $142.3 billion in recent years in information and communication technologies (ICT). This huge investment in ICT should improve China's competitive position in the offshoring service market. Willcocks and Lacity predict that China's IT and business process offshoring service capabilities will be strong.[5] To date, China has managed to attract multinationals such as Accenture, Cap Gemini, Dell, EDS, Hewlett-Packard, and IBM and large Indian-based suppliers like Genpact, Infosys, Satyam, and Tata Consultancy Services to set up captive centers or global delivery centers. China did not develop a strong local vendor market with global foot-prints as India did. Yet the Chinese vendor market continues its evolution. Many Chinese suppliers now want to address the full range of the service value chain rather than compete solely in terms of low-level technical skills. This approach is likely to solidify the technical and managerial skills base of the Chinese market in the coming years.

Despite Chinese optimism, Willcocks and Lacity warn that many client organizations are cautious of China's service base because of language and cultural barriers and concerns over losing intellectual property. The Chinese government and Chinese business sectors are well aware of these barriers and are seeking ways to address them. For example, the Chinese government is investing $5 billion in English-language training to improve the marketability of IT and business process offshoring services from China.

Developing countries outside India and China are becoming stronger players in the IT services market. Many U.S. clients already use Central American suppliers or set up captive centers in this region for Spanish-speaking business processes, such as help desks, patient scheduling, and data entry. Synchronous time zones are one of the obvious drivers for U.S. firms to offshore work to Central or South America. Access to skills and scale are two additional factors that multinationals consider in their assessment of attractive locations. In this regard, Brazil has the advantage of a large population, the innovative creativity of its engineers, and government programs supporting the outsourcing and offshoring industry. Chile and Uruguay have exploited their time zone advantages, back office proficiencies, and government incentives to attract outsourcing and offshoring work.[6]

Willcocks and Lacity also predict that in the coming years, organizations in western Europe increasingly will offshore IT and businesses services to Central Eastern Europe (CEE).[7] Among the key drivers for this trend are proximity to the captive center, limited time zone differences, and lower transaction costs than those incurred by using Asian alternatives. While the CEE region is coming to be seen as an attractive region for nearshoring, our own research reveals a trend in which specific CEE regions, and in some cases even cities, such as Budapest and Sofia, have been considered especially attractive as offshoring locales.

Several countries in sub-Saharan Africa are seeking status among the players in the global IT and business process offshoring markets. These countries, including Botswana and Kenya, have quickly established their economies partly on the competitiveness of IT and IT services.[8] South Africa is exporting IT and business process services, primarily to U.K.-based clients, because of similar time zones, cultural similarities, English-speaking capabilities, and a good infrastructure. Mediterranean North Africa already exports IT services to Europe. The Moroccan IT market is attractive for clients in France because of the common language, similar time zone, and cultural capability.

## Criteria for Selecting Locations

Location selection is one of the major challenges organizations face when making offshoring decisions. A decision to relocate a business function or set up a new captive center facility or delivery center abroad is based to a great extent on the attractiveness of the sourcing locations available.

Several frameworks for selecting offshoring destinations have been posited in the academic and professional literature. These frameworks have been designed to help managers assess the attractiveness of countries and regions. All of these frameworks consider costs, business environment, availability of labor resources, and specific skills. Some frameworks, such as Carmel's eight factors[9] and Farrell's six factors,[10] are more detailed than others (see table 3.1, below) in terms of the factors considered when comparing potential offshoring locations. In our view, the most effective framework currently available is Farrell's six-factor methodology: costs, skills, environment, quality of infrastructure, risk profile, and market potential.[11] We discuss these factors in the following sections and provide an example of how each can be used to compare the attractiveness of several non-BRIC tier 2 countries for the offshoring of IT and business process services. We compare CEE countries such as Romania, Bulgaria, Poland, Slovakia, Czech Republic, and Belarus; Egypt, Morocco, and Tunisia in the Middle East and Africa; Costa Rica and Venezuela in the Americas; and several Asian countries such as Vietnam, the Philippines, and Thailand.

## Costs

Companies considering offshoring IT or business processes services typically compare a range of costs across potential offshoring locations: labor costs (average wages for skilled workers and managers), infrastructure costs (unit costs for telecom networks, Internet access and power, office rent), and corporate taxes (tax breaks, regulations, and other incentives for local investment). In addition, firms are looking at value-added dimensions for how they might benefit over time.

Among the fourteen countries we compared, the highest salaries are in the CEE region. Within CEE, salaries in Slovakia are lower than in Poland and the Czech Republic, although all of three are still significantly lower than in the rest of the EU. This situation is beginning to change as markets change and the skills base develops within particular economies, which has resulted in costs that are increasing more rapidly than those in Asia. One contributing factor to this change is that property prices in CEE vary significantly from area to area. In Prague, for example, monthly rent is on a par with any other Western city. Typically the rent of commercial space in high-tech business parks located near a capital or major city is significantly higher than in more remote business parks, and prime locations within major cities are more expensive than the outskirts. As a result, secondary locations, such as Katowice, Poznan, and Wroclaw, all in Poland, are beginning to emerge in CEE countries; they are close to major universities so as to ensure a supply of skilled graduates while benefiting from the relatively lower property prices offered in such locales.

Labor costs in Morocco are higher than in Tunisia and Egypt, lower than in CEE, and about half the cost of white-collar employees in France. In Tunisia, operation costs are

about 20 percent lower than in Morocco, and in Egypt, wages
are about half those in Morocco. In addition, the rent of commercial space in business parks (called "smart villages") is
significantly lower than in CEE, being on a par with those in
Asia (e.g., the Philippines). As an example, the rent of 1
square meter of office space in Egypt is $180, in India it is
$220, in the Philippines $184, and in Bulgaria $239 (all costs
are in U.S. dollars).

Labor costs in Asia are lower than in all the other countries we have compared, with Vietnam being the cheapest.
Wages in Vietnam are approximately half the average wages
of Indian developers. The costs of telecommunications infrastructure and Internet are relatively low in all the countries
compared, with the exception of Vietnam, which has state-
owned monopolies to control Internet access and keep costs
artificially high. International phone lines in Vietnam are
among the most expensive in the world.[12]

Most CEE countries (apart from Poland, where incentives
are not as high as in the other CEE countries) offer preferen-
tial tax policies and support for investment. Bulgaria and
Slovakia have recently introduced more investment incentives. The Slovak government, for example, introduced new
legislation on investment aid, allowing grants and income
tax relief for IT and shared services centers in the country.
The Romanian government is trying to attract and retain
IT talent by exempting IT professionals from income tax
payment.

Governments in the Middle East and Africa, Asia, and the
Americas offer even higher incentives than CEE countries
do. Some provide complete tax exemption. For example, the
Philippines offers a four- to eight-year income tax holiday,
Tunisia offers tax exemptions on the export of IT-enabled

services, and Morocco offers full exemption for five years and a 50 percent reduction after that.

## Skills

This factor is about the skill pool (size of the labor force with required skills) and vendor landscape (size of the local sector providing IT services and other business functions). Required skills may include technical and business knowledge, management skills, languages, and the ability to learn new concepts and innovate.

The scalability of labor resources in the long term is a major issue to consider when deciding on an offshoring destination. One indication of the scalability of labor resources is the growth in the number of university graduates with desired skills that the target country is able to produce from year to year. Countries that offer high scalability of labor resources are also more likely to keep wages relatively low due to a constant supply of graduates.

Companies that are considering expanding offshore must evaluate the gap between desired and available skills in the target workforce. They should assess the efforts being made by various stakeholders to bridge such skill gaps, for example, through various specialized in-house training programs.

Multinationals looking to set up a captive center must evaluate the vendor's landscape in terms of the skills set (or capabilities) and competencies of offshore vendors. In this regard, they should assess vendors' ability to respond to changes in the captive center's sourcing strategy, with particular attention to their capabilities should the captive center evolve into a shared model. Countries that have suppliers able to demonstrate such competencies to clients are in a better position to attract multinationals and perform both low-value and high-value complex, knowledge-intensive activities. In this regard, the vendor's' landscape combines both local vendors and international suppliers that have a presence in the country, for example, by setting up a delivery center.

The education systems in CEE countries have developed extremely well. They are strong in the sciences, technology, and engineering and accessible to the vast majority of the population. Under communist rule, secondary education was compulsory for the entire population of these former Soviet satellite countries. In contrast, in the Middle Eastern, African, Asian, and South American countries we have examined, a large part of the population still lives in rural areas and is not well educated. The level of literacy in these countries is significantly lower than in CEE countries. Therefore, while CEE countries are on average much smaller in population than Egypt, the Philippines, Venezuela, Thailand, Vietnam, and Morocco, the percentage of the population being educated and becoming highly skilled is much higher.

While CEE countries have a highly skilled workforce with technical skills and training in research and applied sciences, the skilled labor pool is limited in size. For example, Poland, the biggest country with the largest labor pool in CEE, has only 40,000 graduates per year, in contrast with Egypt, which has 330,000 (from all disciplines). Yet only 31,000 of Egypt's students graduate with technology, science, or engineering degrees. Similarly, the Philippines has 380,000 graduates annually, but only 15,000 are focused on technology studies. The main advantage in the skills base that Egypt and the Philippines offer lies in the variety of language capabilities within both countries. English is the main language offered by the Philippine workforce, and the Egyptian labor pools speak a variety of European languages. The impact of this continuous stream of well-educated graduates is that their annual supply of multilingual talent ensures stability in labor costs and a choice of skills and languages for local and international labor markets.

One key challenge that all fourteen countries—Belarus, Bulgaria, Costa Rica, Czech Republic, Egypt, Mexico, Morocco, Philippines, Poland, Romania, Slovakia, Tunisia, Venezuela, and Vietnam—face, however, is a significant lack of management skills—in particular, project management. Setting up a captive center in these countries will mean that the multinational firm will need to transfer management skills or procure those from an international vendor through an insourcing arrangement.

### Environment
This factor encompasses governance support (policy on foreign investment, labor laws, bureaucratic and regulatory burden, level of corruption), the business environment (compatibility with prevailing business culture and ethics), the living environment (overall quality of life, prevalence of HIV infection, serious crime per capita), and accessibility (travel time, flight frequency, time difference).

Governments try to attract foreign investment, and some offer special development zones such as the free trade zone in Egypt, the offshore programming zone in Belarus, and the nearshore center in Morocco. These free trade zones offer tax breaks, less complex administrative procedures, and, in some cases, more flexible labor rules. These investment incentives might be appealing to Western firms, but corruption remains a problem in many of the second- and third-tier countries. The EU, for example, has been monitoring corruption in its member states to ensure that local governments fight this phenomenon.

In terms of business environment, CEE countries are the most attractive destinations for European companies looking to develop nearshore business processes or services through a captive center. Culturally CEE countries provide a good fit with other Western cultures, the time zone difference is limited, and most destinations are easily accessible by air or ground transportation.

Countries in Asia and the Americas require longer travel times and offer wider time zone differences for clients based in Europe. For call centers that operate 24/7, time zone differences do not necessarily create major challenges; however, for offshoring projects that involve software development and the collaboration of globally distributed teams in a number of captive centers, time zone differences may pose coordination challenges.

For North American clients, CEE countries provide a reasonable cultural fit. However, in terms of travel time and time zone differences, these countries can be too remote, and alternative destinations, such as countries in Central America or the Caribbean area, are more attractive.

In terms of the living environment, this factor mainly affects the attractiveness of the offshoring destination for expatriates. This is particularly common in cases in which the client establishes a presence in a destination country in the form of a captive center or as support provided to the vendor's service team. In this regard, CEE countries, where the standard of living is relatively high and there is a cultural fit with Western countries, are the most attractive for expatriates.

## Quality of Infrastructure
Quality of infrastructure refers to telecommunication and IT (network downtime, speed of service restoration,

connectivity), real estate (availability and quality), transportation (scale and quality of road and rail networks), and power (reliability of power supply).

CEE countries are rapidly catching up with Western European countries in terms of the quality of telecommunications and IT infrastructure. Bulgaria, the Czech Republic, and Slovakia, for example, have an excellent telecommunication infrastructure. Romania's domestic telecom infrastructure is still poor but it is improving. The government is seeking to transform Romania into the Internet hub of the Black Sea region, and in the past few years, the country has witnessed one of the largest growths in mobile communications in Europe.

In contrast to CEE, where the quality of telecommunications and IT infrastructure is comparable across countries, the availability and quality of telecommunications and IT infrastructure vary significantly among non-CEE countries. It is common to find advanced IT infrastructures in business parks and large cities, but no or a limited IT infrastructure in rural areas. This situation is prevalent in Tunisia and Morocco. In contrast, the Philippines has an advanced telecommunications infrastructure in large cities and among and between the numerous islands.

Transportation systems in CEE are considered to be advanced compared with other regions. Roads in CEE are in fairly good condition, and most public transport systems consist of rail, metro, and buses. Countries in Asia, the Middle East and Africa, and the Americas have developed transportation infrastructures around areas where a workforce with the required skills is available, often near international airports and major cities. Such high-tech islands are usually surrounded by slums or a desert, provide a high-quality IT infrastructure, have good roads, and offer high-quality office space and other facilities, such as cafeterias and fitness facilities. However, the workforce in these countries mainly relies on private transportation, typically company buses that collect staff in the morning and take them back at the end of the workday. Western visitors typically need a car and a driver to get around. This situation, which seems rather negative compared to CEE, is not different from India in any respect and does not prevent Western counterparts from visiting local facilities. Hotels and company-owned houses offer high-quality living standards for visitors from the West. Companies own cars and employ drivers (and interpreters if needed) to ensure the transportation and communication needs of foreign clients or staff are satisfied. Such arrangements for living and working compensate for the poor transportation system and infrastructure in the rest of the country.

**Risk Profile**
This factor assesses security issues (risks to personal security and property-related issues such as fraud, crime, and terrorism), disruptive events (risk of labor uprising, political unrest, natural disasters), regulatory risks (stability, fairness, efficiency of legal framework), macroeconomic risks (cost inflation, currency fluctuation, and capital freedom), and intellectual property risk (strength of data and intellectual property protection regimes).

Western multinationals see the CEE countries, particularly those that have recently joined the EU, as safer to live in and visit than countries in the Middle East, Africa, some countries in Asia, and even some in the Americas. The Czech Republic, for example, is considered one of the most stable postcommunist countries in the region. Furthermore, CEE countries have suffered less from natural disasters than countries in Asia and the Americas. Flooding in Prague in 2002 caused minor damage compared with the damage caused to Thailand and its population following the 2004 earthquake in the Indian Ocean, which hit Thailand through a series of devastating tsunamis.

Terrorist attacks also affect the attractiveness of a country for trade to the business community. For example, Egypt's image has been damaged as a result of the rare terrorist attacks on the resorts of Dahab in April 2006 and Sharm el-Sheikh in July 2005. There is a perception in some quarters, notably the United States, that Egypt is unsafe, which clearly affects whether it is chosen as a business destination. The Egyptian government is trying to reverse this perception by enforcing security measures, with cars and packages being thoroughly checked and people being searched for weapons or explosives at entrances to office buildings and hotels. In fact, a recent survey of 448 outsourcing users by Black Book Research rated Cairo as the world's tenth safest outsourcing city in 2008. Cairo was preceded by Singapore, Dublin (Ireland), Santiago (Chile), Krakow/Warsaw (Poland), Toronto (Canada), Prague/Brno (Czech Republic), Budapest (Hungary), Monterrey (Mexico), and Beijing (China). When it came to the most dangerous outsourcing locations, the survey listed Jerusalem (Israel), Mumbai (India), and Rio de Janeiro/São Paolo (Brazil) as the top three. This survey was conducted a month before the Mumbai attacks in 2008.

Piracy, intellectual property protection, and copyright laws that affect country attractiveness for trade and out-sourcing are issues of concern. In Venezuela the software piracy rate is above 80 percent. Vietnam, which has a stable and secure environment, is nevertheless known for its exten-sive illegal copying of software and a culture of software piracy. In CEE, Poland and Romania are known for piracy and a lack of intellectual property rights (IPR) protection. Many governments, including Romania, Costa Rica, and the Philippines, are taking steps to strengthen and enforce intellectual property rights protection and copyright laws. In Poland, however, the government has not make any great effort to fight piracy.

**Market Potential**
Market potential can be assessed based on the attractiveness of the local market (current GDP and GDP growth rate) and access to nearby markets (in the host country and adjacent regions). This factor is relevant to captive centers because it indicates whether the parent firm can envisage a growth strategy for the captive center over time. A weak local market potential implies the captive center will very likely remain in its basic form.

CEE countries present a huge market potential. This market is growing as CEE countries become more Western and the quality of life improves, edging ever closer to Western standards. Local CEE demand for software and IT-related products and services is expected to continue to grow.

At present, local markets in the Middle East and Africa are less attractive for Western companies as compared with local markets in CEE. While Morocco and Tunisia focus on French- and Spanish-speaking countries to attract captive centers, Costa Rico and Venezuela mainly attract U.S. companies that are more concerned with proximity to the United States and with costs, while paying little attention to local and neighboring markets. Venezuela, for example, is one of the smallest markets in Latin America and therefore not considered a promising market for the future.

In Asian countries like Vietnam and the Philippines, demand for software and IT-related products and services from the local market is growing, but much more slowly than in CEE. This demand mainly comes from the major cities.

The A.T. Kearney Global Locations Index shown in table 3.1 illustrates a different approach to assessing the attractiveness of a location for offshoring. Their approach provides a score for each factor—financial attractiveness, people skills and availability, and business environment—which are then summed up to create a final composite score. We believe that a qualitative assessment should be combined with a quantified approach to decide on the attractiveness of a location for outsourcing.

### Nearshoring

Nearshoring is an activity in which a client outsources work to a supplier or moves work to a captive center located in a foreign low-wage country that is close in distance and in terms of time zone differences. Compared to offshore outsourcing, the benefits of nearshoring include lower travel costs, fewer time zone differences, and closer cultural compatibility. Canada and Panama, for example, are significant nearshore destinations for U.S. clients. Indeed, U.S. clients can have lower costs when nearshoring work to Canada than by offshore outsourcing to India. As Carmel and Abbott argue, "Distance still matters," and they point to customers choosing the nearshore option in order to benefit from one or more of the following constructs of proximity: geographic, temporal, cultural, linguistic, economic, political, and historical linkages.[13] Their study identifies three major global nearshore clusters based around clients in North America, Western Europe, and East Asia, though this last is a smaller cluster.

**Table 3.1**
A.T. Kearney Global Services Location Index, 2009

| Rank | Country | Financial attractiveness | People skills and availability | Business environment | Total Score |
|------|---------|--------------------------|-------------------------------|----------------------|-------------|
| 1 | India | 3.13 | 2.48 | 1.30 | 6.91 |
| 2 | China | 2.59 | 2.33 | 1.37 | 6.29 |
| 3 | Malaysia | 2.76 | 1.24 | 1.97 | 5.98 |
| 4 | Thailand | 3.05 | 1.30 | 1.41 | 5.77 |
| 5 | Indonesia | 3.23 | 1.47 | 0.99 | 5.69 |
| 6 | Egypt | 3.07 | 1.20 | 1.37 | 5.64 |
| 7 | Philippines | 3.19 | 1.17 | 1.24 | 5.60 |
| 8 | Chile | 2.41 | 1.20 | 1.89 | 5.50 |
| 9 | Jordan | 2.99 | 0.91 | 1.59 | 5.49 |
| 10 | Vietnam | 3.21 | 1.02 | 1.24 | 5.47 |
| 11 | Mexico | 2.48 | 1.50 | 1.45 | 5.43 |
| 12 | Brazil | 2.18 | 1.83 | 1.37 | 5.39 |
| 13 | Bulgaria | 2.83 | 0.89 | 1.62 | 5.34 |
| 14 | United States | 0.47 | 2.71 | 2.15 | 5.33 |
| 15 | Ghana | 3.26 | 0.70 | 1.36 | 5.32 |
| 16 | Sri Lanka | 3.13 | 0.95 | 1.17 | 5.25 |
| 17 | Tunisia | 2.86 | 0.91 | 1.45 | 5.22 |
| 18 | Estonia | 2.06 | 0.93 | 2.20 | 5.19 |
| 19 | Romania | 2.63 | 0.91 | 1.58 | 5.12 |
| 20 | Pakistan | 3.12 | 1.08 | 0.91 | 5.11 |
| 21 | Lithuania | 2.31 | 0.81 | 1.99 | 5.11 |
| 22 | Latvia | 2.28 | 0.86 | 1.96 | 5.10 |
| 23 | Costa Rica | 2.67 | 0.89 | 1.50 | 5.07 |
| 24 | Jamaica | 2.77 | 0.79 | 1.49 | 5.06 |
| 25 | Mauritius | 2.32 | 0.95 | 1.77 | 5.04 |
| 26 | Senegal | 3.06 | 0.88 | 1.08 | 5.03 |
| 27 | Argentina | 2.47 | 1.34 | 1.21 | 5.02 |
| 28 | Canada | 0.54 | 2.10 | 2.38 | 5.02 |

**Table 3.1**
(continued)

| Rank | Country | Financial attractiveness | People skills and availability | Business environment | Total Score |
|------|---------|--------------------------|-------------------------------|---------------------|-------------|
| 29 | United Arab Emirates | 2.10 | 0.84 | 2.04 | 4.98 |
| 30 | Morocco | 2.62 | 0.93 | 1.42 | 4.97 |
| 31 | United Kingdom | 0.43 | 2.13 | 2.39 | 4.94 |
| 32 | Czech Republic | 1.74 | 1.14 | 2.07 | 4.94 |
| 33 | Russia | 2.39 | 1.45 | 1.08 | 4.92 |
| 34 | Germany | 0.42 | 2.10 | 2.40 | 4.91 |
| 35 | Singapore | 0.72 | 1.55 | 2.62 | 4.90 |
| 36 | Uruguay | 2.46 | 1.00 | 1.43 | 4.89 |
| 37 | Hungary | 1.95 | 1.01 | 1.92 | 4.88 |
| 38 | Poland | 1.82 | 1.22 | 1.73 | 4.77 |
| 39 | South Africa | 2.28 | 1.02 | 1.44 | 4.74 |
| 40 | Slovakia | 2.05 | 0.94 | 1.75 | 4.73 |
| 41 | France | 0.40 | 2.03 | 2.29 | 4.72 |
| 42 | Ukraine | 2.63 | 0.97 | 0.99 | 4.58 |
| 43 | Panama | 2.48 | 0.70 | 1.40 | 4.58 |
| 44 | Turkey | 2.01 | 1.23 | 1.29 | 4.54 |
| 45 | Spain | 0.57 | 1.90 | 2.00 | 4.47 |
| 46 | New Zealand | 1.12 | 1.18 | 2.15 | 4.45 |
| 47 | Australia | 0.42 | 1.62 | 2.22 | 4.26 |
| 48 | Ireland | 0.27 | 1.56 | 2.26 | 4.09 |
| 49 | Israel | 0.85 | 1.39 | 1.78 | 4.02 |
| 50 | Portugal | 1.00 | 1.00 | 1.97 | 3.98 |

*Note:* The weight distribution for the three categories is 40:30:30. Financial attractiveness is rated on a scale of 0 to 4, and the categories for people skills and availability, and business environment are on a scale of 0 to 3.
*Source:* A.T. Kearney

The Czech Republic, Poland, and Hungary are important nearshore destinations for Western Europe. Clients in Western Europe are attracted to CEE suppliers for the same reasons that clients from the United States are attracted to suppliers from Canada. Some of the drivers are common language, cultural understanding, minimal time zone differences, and low labor costs. However, central and eastern Europe may be more attractive for business process outsourcing than IT outsourcing; these countries provide the benefits of an excellent general education, but have not produced IT graduates at anything near the rate of India.

We believe that nearshoring in the coming years is less likely to dominate the offshoring strategy. In our opinion, nearshoring will be only one component within the best-shoring strategy, in which each business process is outsourced or offshored based on skills available and cost base offered in the destination.

Finally, it is imperative to consider the influence of certain cities on potential offshoring destinations. Costs, availability of skills, and infrastructure may vary significantly across cities within the same country. Even factors such as environment, risk profile, and market potential can present varying results when examined in each city of the same country. The Global Services Tholons Report by Vashistha and Khan argues that comparing countries is superficial because "no two cities of a country would be at the same level of skills maturity or offer the same cost advantage."[14] For example, some cities graduate more engineers, others more accountants. Therefore, good offshoring decisions are based on an assessment of the attractiveness of potential locations on a city level rather than by country.

Farrell has proposed an approach to assessing city attractiveness for offshoring in which the scale and quality of workforce, business catalyst, cost, infrastructure, risk profile, and quality of life are among the more critical factors for analysis.[15] Vashistha and Khan's comparison of a large number of cities identifies the top eight global outsourcing cities: Dublin, Ireland; Makati City, Philippines; and six cities in India.

## Conclusion

While we have reviewed the main factors that affect country attractiveness for offshoring and illustrated the comparative advantages among the main offshoring destinations through examples, the selection of an offshoring destination remains complex and high risk. A case in point is illustrated in chapter 10 on InfoTech. After setting up a captive center in Budapest, InfoTech had to migrate some of the low-value tasks to a center in Sofia. This example will demonstrate that the context of the sourced tasks also matters. As context changes, the attractiveness of a particular location may change as well.

# 4   Trends in Captive Centers of Fortune Global Firms

This chapter investigates some of the trends among Fortune Global 250 firms regarding their captive centers. These trends can be analyzed by asking three relevant questions:

1. Which Global Fortune 250 companies have captive centers in offshore locations, what types of captive centers are they, and where are they located?

2. Which key location choice criteria do Fortune 250 companies take into account when deciding where to locate their captive centers?

3. Which Global Fortune 250 companies have expanded or migrated their captive centers, and to which locations?

## Study Method and Research

This part of the study focuses on the development of captive centers between 1990 and 2009.[1] A two-stage study of off-shore captive centers ensued to address the three research questions. First, in early 2008, we launched a study into the types of captive centers set up by a sample of the Fortune Global 250. This phase used multiple research methodologies, including twenty-six telephone interviews with senior managers and experts involved in offshoring and scanning articles from the professional media for information about captive centers.

A typology of captive center strategic options emerged that consists of the following types of captive centers: basic, shared, hybrid, divested, terminated, and migrated.[2] Data collected during the first phase also suggested that captive centers evolved. As a result, in early 2009, a second phase was launched consisting of an in-depth study of the evolutionary path of five captive centers owned or formerly owned by Fortune 250 firms in an effort to understand how and why captive centers evolve and generate their own evolutionary path. These case studies are described in chapters 5 through 10. Twenty-five interviews were held with senior managers from the parent firms and the captive centers, focusing on the development path of captive center strategies.

We chose to supplement the expert interviews with an extensive desk research method in order to verify information provided by the experts. The 250 largest firms worldwide, the Global Fortune 250, comprise the sample used in this desk research. Within this sample, we studied the offshoring activities and the location choice criteria for selecting each captive center location. We also used information gathered through desk research and interviews to explore evolving trends in captive center strategies, expansion and migration, and location preference. The desk research involved screening hundreds of articles from which detailed information, such as industry, number of captive centers, and location choice criteria, was recorded.

Our search for information was guided by our definitions of captive center strategies. However, during our research, we identified a need to extend the notion of captive center migration and therefore have taken into account the concept of captive center expansion. As discussed in chapter 2, migration takes place only when captive center operations are physically moved from one location to another. In other words, for a captive center to move, it must first be closed down. Outsourcing the same processes to a third party, for instance, does not meet the criteria for migration in this study. In contrast, the expansion of captive centers implies that the number of captive centers in operation is simply expanded without closing down any captive center location.

Finally, outsourcing location decision theory is both used and tested in order to determine and explore the underlying variables that influence a company's choice of a particular captive center location. Graf and Mudambi proposed a conceptual model for location decision with a focus on outsourcing IT-enabled business processes.[3] In the development of this model, former location choice and country attractiveness theory were screened and used to develop the theoretical framework in their study. For our research purposes, we borrowed and adapted Graf and Mudambi's model of outsourcing location decision making.

For confidentiality reasons, some companies preferred to keep certain information internal, and we have done our best to preserve anonymity in the case studies while providing some basis for the source content. Moreover, the reliability of the location choice criteria mentioned in news articles on the Internet must be questioned. Companies often do not reveal to the press the underlying reasons for establishing a captive center. Rather, they often instead put forward the need for more highly qualified personnel as opposed to cost savings as the reason for offshoring certain tasks abroad in order to garner favorable public opinion. There has been vigorous debate about job losses in the Western world due to multinational enterprises' (MNEs) seeking to lower costs by basing these centers abroad. This could make businesses hesitant to truthfully communicate cost-based reasoning for establishing captives abroad.

## Fortune Global 250 Captive Center Overview

### Captive Centers per Industry

Our research between 1990 and 2009 revealed that Global Fortune 250 companies established 367 captive centers worldwide. These centers were owned by 137 companies (54.8 percent). Furthermore, 77 of these companies own more than one captive center. Extreme examples of this are companies such as IBM, which owns global delivery centers at 18 locations worldwide, and Dell, which owns 11 captive centers. It is worth noting that companies that did not own a captive center often leveraged labor arbitrage and access to qualified personnel by means of offshore outsourcing to a service provider abroad, which is often cheaper than establishing a captive center. Figure 4.1 presents an overview of the number of captive centers per industry. However, as figure 4.2 shows, industry division is not evenly distributed.

Our research also shows that 12.2 percent (45 captive centers) of the Fortune 250 with captive centers pursued a hybrid strategy (SAP and IBM), 11.8 percent (40 captive centers) evolved into a shared captive center model (Barclays, HSBC, J. P. Morgan Chase, Motorola, and Siemens), 6.2 percent (23 captive centers) divested part or all of the captive center (Citigroup, Unilever, and Deutsche Bank), and 8.7 percent (32 captive centers) terminated their captive centers, mainly call centers (Aviva, Dell, and Santander). We

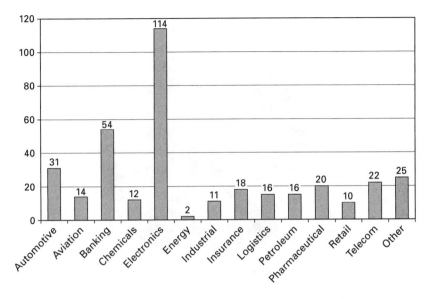

**Figure 4.1**
Captive centers per industry

could not clearly identify the number of captive centers that migrated from one location to another; however, we briefly discuss four cases of captive center migration in this chapter and study in depth another case in chapter 10.

The banking sector, with 48 companies, represents the largest industry among the Global Fortune 250. Other large industries are petroleum, insurance, and electronics, with 29, 27, and 24 companies respectively. Figure 4.3 gives an overview of the number of companies with captive centers per industry.

Accordingly, the banking sector contains the largest number of companies with captive centers. This sector is

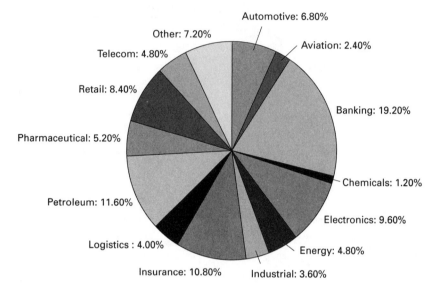

**Figure 4.2**
Industry distribution, Global Fortune 250

followed by the electronics and automotive industries. The petroleum sector, surprisingly, has a very small number of companies with captive centers, as do insurance and retail industries, when compared with their industry representation.

### Captive Centers per Geographic Region

India is by far the most popular destination for captive center development (see figure 4.4). From the 250 companies studied, 115 established captive centers in India, which hosts 146 (39.78%) of the total captive centers identified in this study. The number of captives in eastern Europe and Russia combined is far below those in India, with a total of only 80 captive centers owned by 55 companies. Within this region,

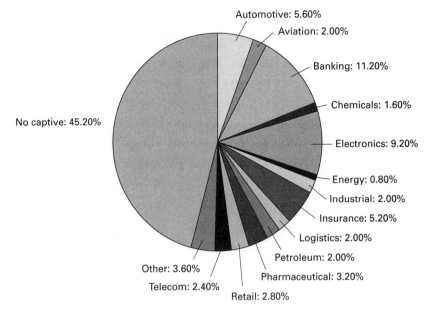

**Figure 4.3**
Captive centers per industry (%)

the most important countries are Poland, Hungary, and the Czech Republic, with 25, 20, and 15 captive centers, respectively.

Countries comprising the "rest of Asia" are Indonesia, Malaysia, the Philippines, Singapore, Sri Lanka, Taiwan, Thailand, and Vietnam. We identified 52 captives owned by 35 companies in this group, most located in Malaysia and Singapore, which host 15 and 21 captive centers, respectively. China alone hosts the same number of captives, 52, as are currently located throughout the rest of Asia.

In the South American region, only 5 captives were identified, and South Africa had only 11, far behind the other

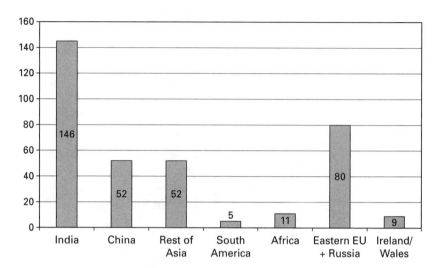

**Figure 4.4**
Captive centers per geographic region

geographic regions presented. Ireland and Wales together
host 9 captive centers, 7 of them located in Ireland.

**Captive Center Activities**

Figure 4.5 shows the division of activities carried out in the
captive centers studied. The graph also displays in which
geographic region the captive activities take place. It should
be noted that out of 367 captive centers, we could not clearly
identify the activities carried out in 83 of them.

R&D has the largest share of the overall captive market,
with 103 captive centers. According to the findings, most
R&D captives are based in China, with 33 captives in that
country alone. India is close behind, with 29 R&D captives,
followed by Eastern Europe and Russia. Combined service
centers (CSCs) are captives that host a variety of offshored

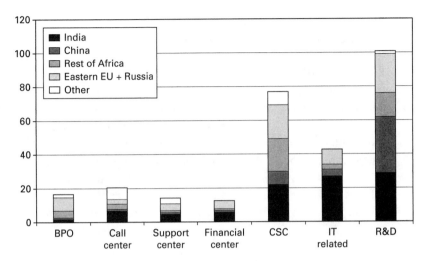

**Figure 4.5**
Activities per geographic region

activities within one unit. These activities rank second among captive center activities, with 77 captives providing services in that category. IT-related captives rank third, with 44 captives, of which more than 60 percent are located in India.

Our research shows that business process outsourcing (BPO) activities were carried out by captive centers owned by companies such as by IBM and Hewlett-Packard, which also carry out BPO activities for third parties. The total number of captive centers hosting BPO, call center, support center, and financial center activities is rather small, however. The Chinese share of this captive market is minuscule in comparison with their mastery of the R&D captive sector. These findings are in line with the Offshoring Research Network (ORN) survey conducted at Duke C.I.B.E.R University in 2008, which demonstrated that R&D was the preferred activity to offshore during 2008. The study also confirms that the Chinese share of R&D captive activities has increased significantly over the last few years.[4]

## Location Choice

In our research, we discovered that the main reason for Global Fortune 250 companies to set up a captive center in a particular location concerns access to human capital, wherein the availability of qualified and talented personnel is the single most important reason given by companies (figure 4.6). A survey we conducted among 263 chief information officers and chief financial officers in Europe confirms that the main driver for offshoring in 2009 was the search for talent.[5]

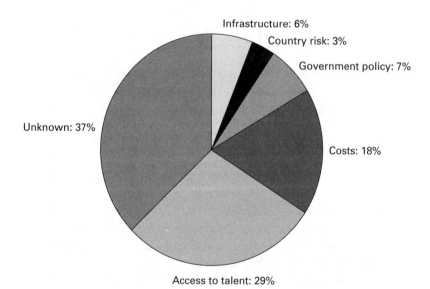

**Figure 4.6**
Location criteria

Government policy and infrastructure were second in importance when assessing potential captive center locations. Country risk was least important and was strongly associated with decisions to set up a captive center in eastern Europe. When considering these factors in the context of key geographic regions, the availability of qualified personnel was important with respect to locating in India and China, but less important in eastern Europe/Russia and the rest of Asia. Government policies and infrastructure were important factors for locating in China, eastern Europe/Russia, and the rest of Asia—more so than its influence in India.

Our research showed other, albeit less significant, factors that affected a company's decision to locate a captive center in a particular location. For example, it is more convenient for companies to have their captive center operations in a time zone close to that of the home country. Conversely, some companies establish their captive center operations according to the follow-the-sun principle, which makes a twenty-four-hour operation possible. Furthermore, many companies prefer to establish a captive center in a country with a significant local market. R&D captives in India and China, for example, also carry out research for local markets. Ties with universities, production facilities in the target country, or a long history in the country are other factors that the companies examined in this research noted. Ultimately time zone and local market considerations are the most significant of these other criteria cited as being important in our study sample.

### The Evolution of Establishing Captive Centers

Companies started to establish captive centers in the early 1990s. Motorola built its first captive R&D center in India in 1990, followed by Citigroup in 1992, which established a

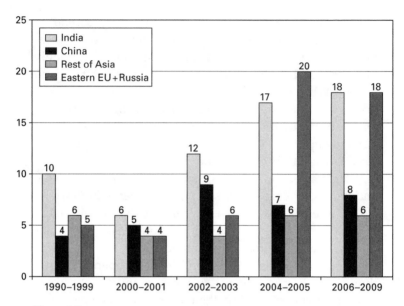

**Figure 4.7**
Newly established captive centers per period and region

major captive operation in the country to carry out financial activities. Microsoft set up an R&D center in Israel in 1991, and in the same year, Canon transferred R&D activities to its new captive center in the Philippines. Figure 4.7 presents an overview of the number of captive centers newly established by the Global Fortune 250 in four geographic regions between 1990 and 2009. The number of newly established captives has increased significantly over the years. Prior to 2004, India was the top destination for new captives; from 2004 until 2009, the eastern European/Russian region overtook the top spot.

The rise in the establishment of captives in the eastern European and Russian region is mainly due to the accession of new eastern European members to the EU and the rapid economic development recently experienced in these countries. In 2004, Cyprus, the Czech Republic, Estonia, Hungary, Latvia, Lithuania, Malta, Poland, Slovakia, and Slovenia joined the EU, followed by Bulgaria and Romania in 2007. China reached its peak during 2002–2003, and the number of newly established captive centers in the country decreased in the subsequent periods. The number of captive centers in the rest of Asia was more or less stable throughout the period studied.

Figure 4.8 shows the different captive center types established between 1990 and 2009. The overall number of R&D

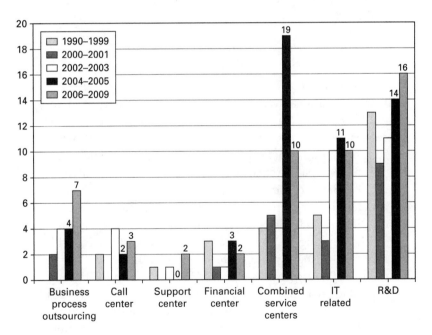

**Figure 4.8**
Number of captive centers by specialization per period

captives increased at a steady pace from 2000 through 2009. IT-related activities demonstrated a significant rise during the periods 2000–2001 and 2002–2003; thereafter, the number of newly established IT captives fluctuated slightly.

In contrast, the number of CSCs skyrocketed during 2004–2005, then subsequently plunged. Nevertheless, from 2006 to 2008, the number of new CSCs being established remained significant, demonstrating a more than 200 percent increase over 2002–2003. BPO captives showed stable, steady growth. The number of newly established financial captive centers and support centers in this study does not show a discernable or explainable pattern from the data gathered.

### Captive Center Trends: What Happens and Where

### Industry Analysis

Establishing a captive center continues to be part of many outsourcing strategies for multinational firms. In particular, companies in banking and the electronics industry own a significant number of captive centers abroad. Extreme examples are companies such as IBM, with ten captive centers in more thirteen countries. Other corporations with a significant number of captives are Royal Philips Electronics, Motorola, Siemens, Hewlett-Packard, and Intel.

The banking industry is the second largest sector, with fifty-four of the captive centers found in this study. In the early 1990s, large banks such as HSBC, ING, and Citigroup started to offshore various activities to India. General Motors was one of the first in its industry to establish a software development captive in India in 1996. Most captive centers carry out R&D work and were largely set up from 2000 onward. The three most important industries with captive centers are electronics and computing (hardware and software), banking, and automotive.

## Electronics and Computing

Increasing globalization has spurred the growth of offshoring in the electronics industry, especially with respect to R&D. The rapid progress of technology development, as well as dramatic cost and price advantages, have been the primary driving force behind MNEs in the electronics industry in setting up an increasing number of R&D captive centers in developing countries. In addition to having access to a large pool of highly educated and skilled English-speaking people, the availability of competent education systems and low cost are the crucial factors driving the number of R&D captive centers in developing regions. Almost half of the captive centers identified in the electronics industry consist of R&D captive centers. Matsushita Electric Industrial opened an R&D facility in China in 2001; a year later, it opened another facility in Singapore, followed by captive R&D centers in Malaysia in 2003 and Vietnam in 2007. These developments mark the beginning of Matsushita's overseas R&D strategy, which leverages talent globally in order to achieve quick turnaround in developing new products. Increasingly companies are establishing R&D locations around the world to leverage talent and react to quickly changing developments in upcoming local markets such as India and China. Extreme examples of this phenomenon are Matsushita, Motorola, and Intel, each with four captive R&D operation facilities.

A large number of shared service centers (SSCs) are identified within the electronics industry. In figure 4.9, SSCs are categorized under the CSC denominator. Siemens is a good

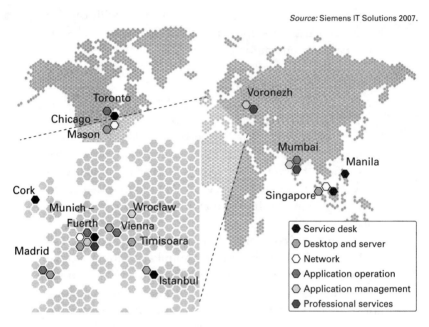

**Figure 4.9**
Siemens's shared service centers

example of a company trying to achieve significant cost savings and consistent service quality by consolidating and standardizing its IT infrastructure into a shared service approach. In its SSC, Siemens carries out accounting and finance activities such as accounts payable and receivable, banking, credit management, credit control, and general accounting. Human resource processes carried out by one of the SSCs include payroll, administration, pension, and travel expenses. A large part of IT infrastructure, including data centers and application management, is processed in another SSC. A mix of international sourcing capacities has ensured long-term global competitiveness for Siemens.

Hewlett-Packard (HP) started its finance and accounting (F&A) SSC journey in 1993 in an effort to reduce operating costs by at least 30 percent within three years. HP also intended to integrate the back-end work of individual business units and countries in order to realize the benefits of consistency in process, operating efficiency, and quality. In 2000, the HP SSC also started to offer F&A outsourcing services to external customers. Today the company provides services to a large number of MNEs from eleven global business centers located in the Americas, Europe, and Asia. As a result, its F&A SSC operation now serves HP business units in 170 countries in addition to its external customers. This SSC network is truly a global endeavor, with operations in India, Costa Rica, Poland, China, Singapore, Spain, Romania, and Mexico.

In the mid-1990s, IBM began specializing in IT outsourcing by operating clients' computer centers and other technical IT-related activities such as support calls. Over the years, IBM has developed into a full-scale outsourcing service provider. It first tried to build its BPO capacity at different locations around the globe organically; however, in 2000, it changed strategies and decided it could accomplish its goals more quickly by acquiring these capabilities rather than building them in-house. One of IBM's major acquisitions took place in 2004 when the company acquired Daksh, an e-services firm in Gurgaon, India, for an estimated $200 million. At the same time, the company began to offshore many of its own activities to SSCs in India, and its Indian workforce has grown steadily, estimated at 80,000 in 2009. IBM also employs significant numbers of people in China, South Africa, Poland, Hungary, Vietnam, Malaysia, Bulgaria, the Czech Republic, Slovakia, Romania, Russia, Egypt, and Portugal.

## Banking

As with the electronics industry, many companies active in the banking sector have established a large number of captives abroad (figure 4.10). Banks such as Citigroup, which established its first captive center in India in 1992, expanded its presence to facilities in eight other locations in India, employing more than twelve thousand people. Citigroup

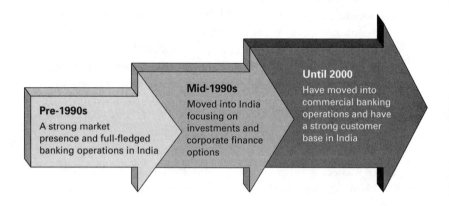

**Early entrants**
- Citibank
- BNP Paribas
- Calyon Bank
- Bank of Nova Scotia
- JPMorgan Chase Bank
- Abu Dhabi Commercial Bank
- Bank of Bahrain and Kuwait
- Taib Bank

**Major banks set up in mid-1990s**
- American Express Bank Limited
- Development Bank of Singapore Ltd.
- State Bank of Mauritius Ltd.
- ABN Amro Bank
- Arab Bangladesh Bank
- DBS Bank

**Major banks set up in 2000**
- Standard Chartered Bank
- Hong Kong and Shanghai Banking Corporation Ltd.
- China Trust Commercial Bank
- Sonali Bank
- ING Vysya Bank

**Figure 4.10**
Banking industry captive centers

also has captive centers in the Philippines, Poland, and Hungary acting as BPO and financial centers. In 2007, however, Citigroup divested its Indian BPO captive operations to Tata Consultancy Services.

HSBC set up its first captive SSC in India in 1995 and today has centers in Hyderabad, Bangalore, Visakhapatnam, Mumbai, Kolkata, and Pune, employing approximately twenty-five thousand people. In 1996, it opened its first captive in China and now has SSCs in Shanghai, Guangzhou, and Shenzhen. In 2004 and 2005, it broadened its captive center network and established facilities in the Philippines, Malaysia, Sri Lanka, and Brazil. Over the years, the London-based bank created a truly global captive operation network and has aligned with a third-party vendor through one of its bank acquisitions.

For a long time, India has been the primary destination for banking sector captives. Early entrants such as Citibank, BNP Paribas, and JP Morgan entered India in the early 1990s. These companies already had a strong market presence in the country and began to leverage their offshoring potential. In the mid-1990s, ABN Amro Bank and others followed suit and established captive operations in India.

Between 2000 and 2002, Lehman Brothers and the Royal Bank of Scotland also opened captive centers in India and started to offshore parts of their noncore IT operations. Cost reductions and the wide availability of qualified personnel were key reasons for choosing India as an offshore destination. However, these banks also saw the huge potential overall for the banking industry in India; through their captive center operations, they gained more insight into the banking industry in that country. Other banks have given the same reasons for establishing captive operations from 2002 onward.

Another essential development among banking institutions is that the activities carried out in their captive operations have moved up the value chain. In the early 1990s, offshored tasks included nontechnical support such as customer care and record keeping. In the mid-1990s, banks started to offshore IT maintenance and software development to their captive centers in India. From 2000 to 2009, core banking activities such as loan processing, credit management, and wholesale banking were partially performed in Indian captives. Today Indian bank captives provide core activities such as investment banking, online trading, asset management, financial research, and analytics. Captive offshoring, which initially began as an experimental endeavor, has become a core competency for many financial institutions. The reasons driving the banking sector's choice of the captive model are directly related to intellectual property and data protection issues. By operating a captive center model, customer data remain in-house; the risk of data misuse and abuse is kept at a minimum, and banks retain control over their best practices and values. Furthermore, this model allows banks to closely monitor and evaluate these processes.

**Automotive**
Approximately one-third of all automotive captive center facilities are located in India. China ranks second, with six captive centers. In 2004, General Motors (GM) established its first auto research and development center in India, its first such facility outside the United States. In 2009, it began construction on an advanced R&D center in Shanghai, China, which will also house the GM Asia Pacific headquarters. The first part of this R&D campus will be fully operational by the end of 2011 and will have more than twenty-five hundred

employees. Kevin Wale, president of GM China, stated that due to soaring fuel prices and stiff competition, the company will spend more of its R&D effort on developing clean energy and fuel-efficient vehicles, which will be the focus of the Shanghai center.

One of GM's reasons for establishing a major R&D hub in Shanghai is that China has become an important market for the company. In 2007, sales in China grew 13 percent, to almost 600,000 GM vehicles sold in the country. Other automotive companies are establishing R&D and engineering facilities in upcoming markets as well. Ford, for example, is pushing more of its IT, manufacturing, and other support operations into growing markets such as India, China, and eastern Europe. Honda, another leader in the industry, has established R&D centers in China, Brazil, Thailand, and Vietnam in order to put more focus on these local markets while leveraging talent globally. German car manufacturer Volkswagen owns R&D facilities in China and India as well, and the company runs a customer interaction center in Uitenhage, South Africa, which won the Global Call Center Awards for 2008.

## Analysis of Captive Centers per Geographic Region

### India

India remains the top location in which Global Fortune 250 companies establish captive operations. This is in line with the findings of the A.T. Kearney GSLI research study.[6] In this study, the consultancy firm points out that India and China dominate the index by large margins. There have been many debates about the decreasing attractiveness of India as an offshoring destination due to an increase in labor costs and high attrition rates. The study shows labor costs in India increased by approximately 30 percent in 2007 alone. Nevertheless, India still offers a good mix of relatively low costs, excellent technical skills, a large English-speaking workforce, and a government that continues to stimulate foreign direct investment.

In order to sustain gains from the lower cost base and a large pool of qualified and available personnel offered by India, companies are increasingly establishing captive operations in tier 2 and tier 3 cities. Jones Lang Lasalle, a world-leading real estate service firm, recently published a report that identified Ahmadabad, Chandigarh, Indore, Kolkata, and Nagpur as the five emerging Indian tier 3 cities best positioned for offshoring IT-related activities over the next five years.[7] According to Vincent Lottefier, country head of Jones Lang LaSalle India, the increasing cost of operating captive facilities in tier 1 cities such as Bangalore, Mumbai, and Delhi, and to a lesser extent in tier 2 cities such as Hyderabad, Chennai, and Pune, has pushed companies toward tier 3 cities to satisfy their cost requirements regarding offshoring business processes. According to their research, these cities provide cost advantages of up to 30 percent in comparison to the tier 1 and tier 2 cities in India because of lower labor and real estate costs and reduced attrition.

The comfort level and ease of setting up captive center facilities in tier 1 and tier 2 cities is often the main reason cited by companies that launch their first captives in the country. For example, Walmart is looking at Bangalore to establish a captive IT center in 2010 to support its growing international business and local operations in India. Barclays Bank also set up BPO operations in 2009, creating five thousand new jobs in India. The company sold its 50 percent stake in its shared BPO to Intelenet Global Services when it decided to create its own captive unit in India instead.

Many scholars consider American Express a best practice model in the area of captive centers. The company started its offshore operations in the 1990s and at that time focused solely on transaction processing, before broadening its scope to include customer service. From its captive center in India, American Express also offers fraud and risk modeling and financial processing to its customers around the globe. Prior to establishing its captive operations in India, American Express had substantial operating experience in the country. From this experience, it knew that transaction costs were approximately 40 percent lower and, even more important, that the quality of output was superior to what they could produce domestically. These observations persuaded American Express management to locate one of its three SSCs in India, mainly servicing the Japan and Asia Pacific regions. American Express also took into account human capital dimensions when making its decision.

**Captive Center Activities in India**    A wide variety of captive activities are carried out in India. Large MNEs began to establish their first captive centers in India in the early 1990s. At that time, only noncore operations such as transaction processing and call center operations were offshored to India. However, offshore activities moved up the value chain over time, and today high-end work is carried out in captive centers throughout India. A significant number of captive centers host R&D activities, IT and IT-enabled services, and, to a slightly lesser extent, a combination of different business process activities.

The wide variety of activities carried out in Indian captive centers is directly related to the broad skill set of the Indian population. Several studies, including the NASSCOM-McKinsey study, researched the status of human power in the country.[8] This study concluded that the number of IT-BPO professionals employed in India grew from 200,000 in 1998, to more than 1.6 million in 2007. This growth was mainly due to the demographic profile of the population and the high-level universities in the country. India has approximately 347 institutes of higher education and almost 17,000 colleges, with more than 10 million students enrolled. These institutions educate around 495,000 technical graduates and nearly 2.3 million other graduates yearly. Compared to other offshore destinations, India has the largest number of qualified offshore talent available at this time.

**Migration of Captive Centers within India**    Migration of captive centers within India is difficult to identify. However, companies are increasingly looking at tier 2 and tier 3 cities to expand their captive network in order to gain an advantage from the lower cost base and more extensive talent pool. HSBC provides a good example of expanding its Indian presence to cheaper locations within the country. The bank established its first captive center in Pune, a satellite city of Mumbai (tier 1), but rising wages forced it to look for alternative locations such as Calcutta. The bank's chief operating officer said in 2005, "India definitely gives us a labour arbitrage when compared with developed countries. However, with increasing cost of employment across all sectors, we will have to look into the labour arbitrage within the country."[9] Today, the company owns captive facilities in Hyderabad (tier 2), Bangalore (tier 1), Visakhapatnam (tier 3), Mumbai (tier 1), Kolkata (tier 2), and Pune (tier 2). Other examples are Bank of America, with centers in Hyderabad (tier 2) and Mumbai (tier 1); Nokia, which owns captives in Bangalore (tier 1), Mumbai (tier 1), and Hyderabad (tier 2);

and Robert Bosch, with captive centers in Bangalore (tier 2), Coimbatore (tier 3), and Saravanampatti (uncategorized).

## China

We identified fifty-one captive centers in China, owned by forty-seven Global Fortune 250 companies. This is in stark contrast to India, where a significant number of companies own more than one captive operation. China ranks second on the A.T. Kearney Global Service Location Index, just behind India. Chinese infrastructure has developed over the years; the number of university students has increased significantly, and the number of companies with capability maturity model integration, which is important for the software industry and ISO quality certifications, has grown dramatically. The standards in China are improving, making the country a more competitive world player.

The Global Services–Tholons Study presents an overview of the top fifty emerging global outsourcing cities.[10] China claims six places on this list, with Shanghai and Beijing ranking second and third, respectively. Shenzhen (tenth), Dalian (sixteenth), Guangzhou (twenty-third), and Chendu (thirty-seventh) are other notable cities on this list. Shanghai is considered a more mature destination for providing service offerings such as F&A, product development, R&D, and testing, and Guangzhou is better known for its engineering service offerings. The Chinese government is also stimulating offshoring by Western firms. This factor, in combination with the emphasis on the English language in Chinese schools, makes China a promising offshoring location in the future.

BASF has been leveraging Chinese talent for a long time. The company has been trading in China since 1885 and now has twenty-nine wholly owned companies in China, has established nine JVs, owns fourteen production sites, and has more than five thousand employees. China's expertise has shifted over the years from a pure manufacturing base to a growth model of innovations and new technologies. BASF's R&D centers focus on development for the Chinese market, which gives the company access to the latest technologies through close collaboration with the scientific community in China.

Microsoft set up its first R&D center in Asia in 1998 and has grown to more than 350 researchers and engineers. In 2004, its Chinese research lab was awarded the title of "the world's hottest computer lab." Microsoft strives to leverage talent from all over the world and recognizes the importance of China as an area of innovation. Similarly, Pfizer established a clinical trial center in China in 2004 and extended its Global Shared Services network with a captive center in Dalian, China, in 2007. The Dalian Global Financial Shared Service Center is a global operation that delivers standardized processes to its subsidiaries in the Asia Pacific region.

**Captive Center Activities in China**  Approximately 63 percent of all captive facilities in China carry out R&D activities. The second largest group consists of activities carried out in CSCs. Multinational enterprises setting up R&D facilities in China often have production facilities in the country. By establishing R&D centers, these firms are able to focus more on the increasing importance of the domestic Chinese market, the single largest market on the globe.

NEC is one of many companies that followed this strategy and established a software development group within its existing Chinese subsidiary. Tyco International also recently opened an R&D center in Shanghai. The captive center operation will focus on the design and product R&D for Tyco Fire and Security and will leverage local expertise and talent for its knowledge creation globally, but will also focus on the Chinese market: "This new R&D center will let Tyco International create more tailored services for the Chinese market," said Edward Breen, chairman and CEO of Tyco International.

## Rest of Asia

The captive centers that fall into the "rest of Asia" category mainly consist of captive centers in Malaysia functioning mostly as CSCs and contact centers, captives in the Philippines hosting CSCs and a number of call centers, and BPO-related activities throughout the region.[11] Captive center operations in Singapore were also found. A small number of captives were found in Indonesia, Vietnam, Sri Lanka, Taiwan, and Thailand.

Malaysia offers strong government support and continued investment in infrastructure of high quality. The government stimulates programs to expand the labor pool and, more important, encourages its citizens to improve their English-language capabilities and technical skills. The country, however, lacks critical mass, and the service maturity is currently too low at this time to become a first-class IT service location. Shell, however, established its SSC in Kuala Lumpur, Malaysia, in 2000 and started providing F&A services to Shell companies in the Asia Pacific region. In 1997, Shell had already developed Shell Information Technology in Cyberjaya, now the global hub for some of Shell's major IT activities. The company employs more than thirteen hundred people.

In 2007, electronics company Hitachi Data Systems opened a regional contact center in Kuala Lumpur. The center hosts three teams that monitor pricing, configuration, and presales support for the Asian Pacific region. BHP Billiton established a SSC in the same city in 2009 with the goal of obtaining cost and time efficiencies. The Kuala Lumpur center mainly acts as a transactional back office facility for the company's global operations.

The Philippines is a preferred destination among American companies because of the English-language skills available within the population. The country also has one of the best financial government incentives for attracting IT businesses. However, the Philippines lacks a sound infrastructure, and IT process maturity is very low. In 1998, Chevron established an SSC in Makati City and now employs more than one thousand people and provides transactional, processing, and consulting services to its businesses in the Asian Pacific, African, and North American regions. In 2003, JP Morgan elected to locate its captive center in Makati City to process its back office operations. In 2009, the company opened a fourteen-thousand-seat call center in Taguig City. The experience the company has gained over the years has made it comfortable with the business and political climate in the country. Therefore, in addition to India, the Philippines will be the main offshoring destination for JP Morgan. Dell also established its contact center in the country, mainly due to the workforce's strong language and communication skills, as well as its high quality. In 2007 Dell expected the Philippines to become the primary contact center location in Southeast Asia.

Singapore has positioned itself as a location for high-end activities that require optimal intellectual property protection and data privacy. The risk of establishing operations in Singapore is relatively low, and the English proficiency in the country is moderate. The main disadvantage of locating in Singapore is the cost of operations. Strikingly, the country itself has begun to look for other low-cost locations to outsource its own low-end processes in order to save costs. Dell established its Asia Pacific Web Farm in Singapore in 2000, and it has provided better Internet routing for Dell customers trying to access the Web site. The number of activities at the Singapore location has increased over the years, and the Web farm now hosts online stores for Dell customers and a number of other support services. Dell initially chose this location because of the excellent IT infrastructure in the country and the highly trained people available in the region.

### Eastern Europe and Russia

Over the past ten years, the central and eastern European (CEE) region has emerged as one of the main locations, after India and China, for establishing captive centers. Most captive centers in the region are located in Poland, Hungary, and the Czech Republic. The overall number of centers established in this region after 2004 increased rapidly.

The number of newly established BPO operations has increased significantly since 2004. Nevertheless, the CEE still lags behind other regions and counts for only a small part of the world's total IT and BPO offshoring market. However, this is changing as costs in India increase at a rapid pace, and attrition rates in Indian tier 1 and tier 2 cities have a negative influence on service quality.[12] Western European firms in particular have begun looking more and more to Eastern Europe as an alternative nearshoring location. Wages in this region have more or less converged with the wage levels in Indian tier 1 and tier 2 cities. Infrastructure in most CEE countries is reliable, and the geographic proximity and culture are much closer to Western Europe. Furthermore, the availability of qualified personnel in the region is very good:

local universities educate a significant number of graduates every year, and the foreign language capabilities among people make the region an attractive offshoring destination for western European firms.[13]

Honeywell opened its first offshore R&D center in Prague in 1993, in cooperation with the Technical University. Ten years later, the company expanded its presence in the country and opened a global design center and a European manufacturing base in Brno. In 2006, Honeywell opened its Aerospace Business Support Center in Prague, servicing various businesses in Europe, the Middle East, and Africa. Robert Bosch was also among the early entrants into the Czech Republic. The company built a factory and an R&D center in 1992. In 2006, it increased its presence in the country by opening up a development center in České Budějovice, employing more than two hundred highly qualified people. Through these centers, the company is able to leverage the best talent available in the country and gains from a relatively low cost base.

In 1995, Motorola set up its first R&D Center in Poland and recently decided to expand its center in Krakow. Motorola located its R&D captive in a Special Economic Zone, the Kraków Technology Park, which offered the company extra financial incentives to establish its facility at that location. Motorola cites the availability of qualified personnel, excellent logistics, and the central location as reasons for establishing the R&D captive in Krakow.

Citibank established a financial center in Poland in 2005. In 2006, it chose Hungary as the location for one of its IT global service centers. The company already owned a large branch network in the country and was satisfied with the knowledge and skills of the Hungarian workforce. This experience contributed to its decision to establish a captive center in Hungary. Citibank cited the well-developed infrastructure, sound legal environment, stable governance, and competitive cost structure as additional important factors.[14]

In summary, the biggest share of captive centers in CEE host R&D activities, followed closely by captives carrying out CSC activities. BPO and IT-related captive operations are moderately present in this region, with only a small number of financial, support, and call center activities to be found.

## Migration

There is not an abundance of cases identified in our research that demonstrate the migration phenomenon of captive centers, wherein the parent firm moves a captive from one location to another. In our study, we clearly identified four such cases: Deutsche Post World Net, IBM, Dell, and Motorola.

**DPWN/DHL**   Deutsche Post World Net (DPWN), the corporate parent of Deutsche Post AG and DHL, which ranks seventy-fifth on the Global Fortune 250 list in 2010, migrated its scattered IT development and operations model to three consolidated centers in 1997: Cyberjaya, Malaysia; Prague, Czech Republic; and Scottsdale, Arizona, in the United States. Along with support from vendors in India, these facilities keep Deutsche Posts' IT operations and development running around the clock. These facilities are complemented by another application development center in Bonn, Germany.

After a thorough study of many location possibilities, including the Philippines, Perth, Brisbane, Thailand, Malaysia, India, Singapore, and Hong Kong, DHL chose Malaysia as the most central and economical location in which to establish one of its three consolidated IT centers. The business-friendly environment, government incentives, and a skilled and affordable labor pool all factored into DHL's decision to locate in Malaysia.

Prague was not the cheapest location in terms of labor costs, but it was the best in terms of the pool of English speakers, infrastructure, workforce capabilities, and government policy. In this case, cost was not the only factor DHL took into consideration. Attributing such importance to skills and talent as the primary factor can be explained in this case by the higher-end activities performed at this center.

The migration of DHL was not purely a migration from one location to another. It was actually part of its global IT strategy. In order to ensure leverage from the potential economies of scale and improve service quality, DHL decided to consolidate its numerous IT operations, which were scattered around the world. The three location choices enabled DHL to assume a follow-the-sun principle and gave the company more flexibility. Under this global structure, IT applications could be developed much faster, and the time to market was significantly reduced. The intention was to use productivity in order to cut total development time nearly in half. Owing to the time differences between the captive centers and the DHL entity for which a particular IT project is run, errors in any particular system can be solved during nighttime hours and be up and running the following day.

**IBM**   IBM closed an outsourcing hub in India in 2005 that focused on financial services, human resources, procurement, and call center–related activities. At the same time, it opened a new captive operation center employing seven hundred people in Hungary who took over the work of the former captive. The Indian captive was partially sold to an

Indian service provider. IBM pointed out that the main reason for moving its BPO captive to Hungary was the geographic proximity to western Europe, the language skills of the Hungarians, and the lower cost base.

Another reason for migrating the Indian captive center was the negative perception by the U.S. public and politicians on the issue of offshoring jobs to India. There has been a long debate in the United States about native companies' transferring American jobs to low-wage countries—India in particular. However, IBM still has very large operations in India and continues to increase its head count there. According to IBM insiders, the company is mainly seeking to lower its cost base and increase its access to qualified personnel.

**Dell**  Dell India recently moved its hardware R&D unit from Bangalore to Texas and Taiwan, mainly due to the increase in operating costs and insufficient hardware talent pool. It changed its focus in India on software development and testing. The availability of qualified personnel was the deciding factor for moving the R&D captive center out of India. The lack of hardware talent in India fed into an increase in labor costs, forcing up wages for qualified workers. In contrast, Taiwan had a larger pool of hardware talent available at a reasonable cost.[15]

A recent study by Zinnov Management Consultancy revealed that in 2007, just fifteen overseas tech firms opened R&D centers in India compared to seventy-six, seventy, and forty-eight in each of the years from 2004 to 2006. This case lends further evidence to the general findings of our own study: access to qualified personnel and cost levels are key factors in establishing a captive center at a given location, and these factors are also key with respect to the migration of a captive center.

**Motorola**   Motorola transferred its call center operations from Brazil to Argentina in 2004. A.T. Kearney suggests that Brazil has the best people skills in the South American region; however it is not the cheapest.[16] Argentina has better cost advantages but scores lower on business environment and experience with BPO-related services. More information on this migration could not be identified; however, the A.T. Kearney study points to the cost differences between operating a BPO unit in Brazil versus Argentina as the key reason for this migration.

## Conclusion

When companies decide to offshore their activities to captive centers initially and then migrate captives to a different location late, access to skills and talent weighs heavy in the decision making. Labor costs are another factor, but we believe that in the years to come, this factor will no longer dominate firms' decision making regarding their offshoring selection.

This chapter lays the foundation for Part II, which explores the evolution of captive center strategies and capabilities by examining six cases in depth.

# II    Captive Centers in Practice

The chapters in this part analyze the underlying reasons that companies set up captive centers and evolve them into hybrid, shared, divested, or migrated captives through case studies. For each development option within the different strategies, one case study is provided. The case studies were conducted with mainly Indian captives of international companies in 2008 and 2009. To ensure confidentiality and anonymity of the companies and interviewees, names of the companies and the interviewees are not given and pseudonyms are used. We interviewed twenty-five top managers, middle managers, and experts involved in offshoring. Unless another reference is cited, the data and information provided come directly from the interview source. To further ensure confidentiality of our case study participants and sources, all print references to the company provide only a journal title and date of publication.

# 5 From Basic to Hybrid: The Case of GlobalSoftware

The hybrid captive center can be carried out in two forms: as hybrid insourcing or hybrid outsourcing (figure 5.1). In hybrid insourcing, services are provided on the client's premises. Contracting consulting services, where the vendor's personnel physically work from the client's site, is a good example. In hybrid outsourcing, the work is outsourced to a local vendor and performed at the vendor's site. This case describes both scenarios.[1]

## Evolving into a Hybrid Captive

The captive unit of GlobalSoftware, a worldwide leading software development firm, was set up through an acquisition in India in 1998. Today it is the second largest R&D and global services and support center in the world and contributes to all parts of the parent company's value chain. The captive center's geographic scope has expanded to more than eight locations around the globe. The basic unit has evolved into two different hybrid structures, exploiting the strong local vendor market (figure 5.2). First, the captive center evolved into a hybrid insourcing model where the third-party provider became part of the captive center's

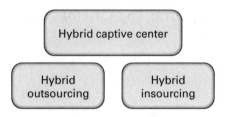

**Figure 5.1**
Hybrid insourcing and outsourcing

team. Then parts of the business operation and services that required seasonal skills were outsourced to providers located outside the captive unit (hybrid outsourcing). This allowed GlobalSoftware to achieve lower costs and flexibility, obtaining the maximum benefits offered by hybrid captive model.

**The Basic Captive Center**

In the late 1990s GlobalSoftware planned to set up a product development center in India. According to the codirector of the captive unit, "India has excellent people, and it is possible to grow very fast." The Internet boom was at its peak, and many IT companies were in dire need of resources. "Therefore, there was an arbitrage of costs, to [a] certain extent, to recruit the people," said the director of process improvement and performance management (PIPM). In 1998, GlobalSoftware acquired a company that provided front-office software for marketing and business operations from its Indian office. The team of the acquired company already had seventy experienced software professionals in place. They immediately started to work on the new sales force automation of the parent software company.

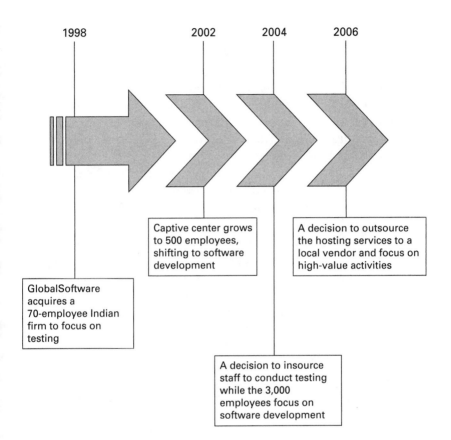

**Figure 5.2**
GlobalSoftware's evolution from basic, to hybrid insourcing, to hybrid outsourcing

Within a few years, the Indian operation was in a position to add activities. The company set up testing operations at the Indian unit because it had "basically the cost advantage and cost [effectiveness]," recalled one manager. The manager of business research extension added, "We are using a number of people coming out of public colleges. So these people are there and they are available. The costs of that model are at least three to four times cheaper than when you set it up in [GlobalSoftware's home country]." By 2002, the captive center employed five hundred software developers and received investments of over $125 million from Global-Software, the parent firm. By 2006, the captive center had increased its capacity to more than three thousand staff, many of them software developers.

The software giant considered its captive unit a part of its back office operations, which handled low-level tasks cheaply. The board of the parent firm made all decisions and prevented the captive center from making recommendations at the portfolio level. The captive unit could only contribute, and to a small extent, to the design and architecture of the processes; it did not have full ownership of, for example, a GlobalSoftware solution. The director of PIPM adds, "If we look at the capabilities of the people, we have maybe ten product managers as a maximum, out of four thousand people. We [were] still in the mode where the definition of the product, and to certain extents, the platform or the archi-tecture, [was] not here."

GlobalSoftware also faced problems with the high attrition rate in India. The director of PIPM succinctly described the problem: "If we have a lot of attrition, we do not get domain knowledge. And if we do not get domain knowledge, we do not get more responsibility. If you have an attrition of 30 percent every two years, you nearly start from zero."

In order to improve the contribution of the captive center to GlobalSoftware's product portfolio, the parent firm's top team acknowledged the need to better integrate the captive center. This meant GlobalSoftware not only had to look into the captive center's position and role within the global strategy, but also at the way the parent company's structure should adapt to meet the needs of integrating the captive center into its worldwide operations. For example, the parent firm designed a stage-gate approach for all of its divisions, which allowed easier data transfer and communication across different business units, including the captive center. This approach also increased the level of formality and standards, permitting managers to synchronize their go or no-go decisions. In addition, the stage-gate approach helped to overcome cultural differences, particularly with respect to captive center employees, mostly Indian, who were not used to disagreement. Thereafter, employees had to base their decisions on the strict requirements of the stage-gate approach and learn to make no-go decisions when appropriate.

While attracting employees was one of the lesser problems faced, the company was not completely immune to attrition problems. GlobalSoftware profited from its strong brand name and its international operational structure, which attracted many potential employees; however; the PIPM director admitted that attrition problems continued. In an attempt to mitigate this issue, the parent company learned to give more responsibility to its captive center staff and offered a broader scope of work, allowing the captive center to move up the value chain. In order to address the issue of cultural differences, the parent firm offered training sessions to the Indian staff regarding cultural attitudes and awareness.

---

*Key motives* Part of take-over; cost savings; gain access to talent pool; 24/7 work; free up staff in home country; increase the innovation level
*Challenges* Cultural differences; attrition rate; gaining higher-value tasks and responsibility
*Solutions* Change structure and cultural attitude; set up training programs; use brand name; move up the value chain

---

## Evolution into a Hybrid Captive Center

In the early days of the basic captive center, testing new software was mainly performed by consultants and customers. Each product required testing since the company's competitive advantage lay in delivering products suited to the needs of each customer. However, the company's consultants preferred to spend 70 percent of their time on sales because their compensation was based on sales volume. This resulted in an inadequate testing period for the center's software. Although customers sent their employees to the software company for applications training, they spent their time learning the new programs, not testing. Hence, "Nobody clearly check[ed] whether the system development [was] according to the customer requirements and specifications," said the director of PIPM.

In 2004, the captive center's top team decided they needed to create more stability in this area. In order to overcome the dearth of testers and contribute to the company's growth potential, they formed a restructuring team to bring in employees and resources from outsourcers to perform noncore functionality testing. As a result, the captive center was able to focus on its main tasks (development) and put aside the problem of attrition rates and attracting skilled labor. Fifty percent of the new staff became full-time captive center employees within twelve to eighteen months, while another 50 percent came in on a short-term basis.

### Hybrid Insourcing Captive

The captive center set up an insourcing arrangement in which the vendor sent in staff with basic programming skills to perform high-quality testing. The captive center trained the new staff on its application and testing procedures for three months before sending them into testing units. After the required time, the new staff were fully integrated into the captive center.

Because software testing generally suffers from business cycles and staffing needs fluctuate significantly, the company benefited from the short-term staff provided by the vendor. In this way, the company was able to attract and accommodate more new customers without struggling with the availability of skilled personnel during business cycles.

While the captive center benefited from this new agility, management still had to deal directly and indirectly with the high attrition rate in this region, which remained a major challenge for both captive center and vendor. Many testers joined the company on a short-term basis in order to gain knowledge about specific software because "they wanted to learn what is hot in the market," recalled one senior manager. However, when they were assigned to other software programs that did not meet their expectations, their motivation suffered, and many testers left. Furthermore, the company had to train the new employees for a minimum of three months before they were assigned to testing groups, regardless of the time they spent on the job. The employees had to learn and adapt to the captive center structure, procedures, and processes, all of them foreign in the Indian context. This resulted in high attrition for the vendor and affected the testing services that the captive center provided.

Addressing some of these challenges was quite difficult for the captive center. The approach taken in the end was to create a partnership with the vendor to ensure the insourced staff would be offered a career path within the partnership. The practical approach was to agree on a fee of 30 percent of the cost of the training paid by the vendor should the insourced employee leave the company within three months. Under this arrangement, the vendor was clearly motivated to reduce the attrition level of its insourced staff. The captive center also developed a network of independent consultants who were mostly previously employed by the vendor. The center benefited from their knowledge in the testing area without having to invest in training.

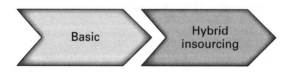

Basic        Hybrid insourcing

*Key motives*  Gain access to talent pool; react to cycles; increase the number of external consultants
*Challenges*  Meet employees' expectations; rely on a centralized testing department
*Solutions*  Develop measurement tools; create profile fits; share risks

## Hybrid Outsourcing Captive

In 2004, the captive center realized growth opportunities and consequently devised strategies to free up staff to focus on higher-value activities. At the parent firm's level, there had been a shift toward research and product and service development. The captive center's top team consequently decided to outsource the hosting and application management, as well as the customer relationship management (CRM) function, because "some of those tasks were quite repetitive and did not add high value," argued the director of PIPM. Nonstandard tasks that focused on interfacing with customers were retained within the captive center. In 2006 the captive center signed an outsourcing contract with a local vendor. By 2007 the center outsourced a dozen services, which were provided by a team of over 120 employees from the vendor firm. The center considered outsourcing additional functions; however, it was still reluctant to outsource any of its nonrepetitive work to a third party because the "[vendor] doesn't know our business. You can't transfer the customer knowledge. Every customer has a different landscape. My people take about six weeks to learn this landscape," claimed one senior manager.

To ensure the best fit between the captive center and the vendor, the captive center performed due diligence with six different vendors. The director of PIPM followed some specific requirements regarding the selection process: "Of course, [the vendors] should have basic capabilities such as the size, while being able to attract two hundred engineers specialized in [certain parts of the software company]." However, he highlights that "all those big Indian service companies are able to attract people and have good names. [In] the end, the decision was based on the question: Can we make sure that we benefit from the relationships and [can] we develop a relationship with the vendor? What will be our relationship two years down the line?" Ultimately the decision came down to the vendor's culture, which was very similar to that of the captive center.

Yet the captive center needed to find a way to clearly define the services it required from its vendor. For this reason, standardized procedures for service quality and product offerings had to be developed from scratch. Clearly the captive center had to make itself outsource-ready quickly. One manager recalled that the captive center "outsourced activities we believed that were standard, but they were not." The impact on the outsourcing relationships in the beginning of the contract was devastating. About half of the outsourced work experienced problems for the vendor, and often the vendor had to request assistance from the client when providing services, a situation that was frustrating for both client and vendor. In the end, the captive center had to acknowledge its responsibility and work with the vendor to stabilize and restore the service.

Another problematic area was the relationship between the vendor and the captive center, which was very restricted in the beginning. The captive center gave only two days of training to the vendor and expected the vendor to provide quality services thereafter. In addition, the vendor faced the same challenges as the captive center with regard to 24/7 work and high attrition rates. There were days that each shift had to be trained individually. Each subsequent employee also needed to receive the same training provided to the initial groups.

The source of the problem was identified in the knowledge transfer methodology and processes. It could be easily attributed to the immaturity level of the captive center in terms of its sourcing management capabilities. The captive center addressed these pitfalls by redesigning its hosting processes, improving the hosting infrastructure and involving the vendor in each change made along the way. New service level agreements (SLAs) were put in place that reflected better on the service portfolio, and a team from the vendor was sent to the captive center for a knowledge transfer phase. The captive center also allocated staff to work with the vendor's teams to provide constant support and training. Finally, the captive center developed metrics to measure performance—something rarely done when services were delivered from the captive center.

Key motives    Focus on core activities; focus on high-value activities; achieve cost savings
Challenges    Standardize processes; build up sourcing relationships; change management
Solutions    Provide additional training for the vendor; redesign outsourced processes; improve contract management; develop metrics

### Short-Term Hybrid Outsourcing Captive

A third outsourcing option for the captive center is project outsourcing, which relates to tasks that occur occasionally for a short period of time. According to one manager, "Very often this kind of outsourcing is not for services, but it is for developing a product." The captive center outsourced projects for product development whenever it lacked the knowledge or capabilities. The captive center had to enter due diligence phases with potential vendors and realize which capabilities the vendor possessed and where those capabilities were suitable for the task. Cooperation with a vendor required the captive center to clearly define who would lead the project and who would have ownership of the licenses. In addition, the captive center had to learn how to share information with an external vendor regarding some sensitive strategic objectives, in particular, when the relationships were set up to address a short-term project. The captive center's approach was to set up a revenue-sharing agreement to secure the ownership of the intellectual properties and income. The underlying principle in this approach was that the captive center saved time but not money.

Following this outsourcing agreement, the captive center was able to deliver services and products to customers, though the knowledge and capabilities were extracted from an external vendor. As a result, the captive center's reputation for providing up-to-date solutions grew, and some of the solutions that the external vendor developed were diffused across the parent firm. By obtaining these services through outsourcing relationships, the captive center avoided the need to develop this knowledge in-house, as it was obvious the local vendor market was populated with advanced and sophisticated vendors. Furthermore, the captive center employees were given an excellent opportunity to learn about different technologies and sourcing management practices from these short-term partnerships.

Although the captive center benefited from the capabilities provided by the vendor, it still faced some challenges. One key challenge was the unit's ability to select the most suitable vendor for this type of short-term engagement. The captive center did not possess advanced sourcing management expertise and resources were scarce; therefore, using intermediaries to facilitate the vendor selection process was not an option. The captive center also had to ensure that although its own staff were not actively involved in the product development, they still engaged, learned, and maintained a high degree of involvement. Clearly, maintaining this level of motivation was also a concern. Finally, the captive faced a major challenge in striking a balance between a productive knowledge-sharing atmosphere between the vendor and client teams and protecting its intellectual property without hampering the relational aspects.

The captive center applied an approach based on three pillars: develop trust, work with multiple vendors, and engage employees in outsourcing. More simply, the captive center preferred to develop trust with its vendors as the main vehicle to achieve high performance and results, while relying on the contract as a risk-mitigation mechanism. Therefore, sharing knowledge between vendor and client teams was perceived to be of higher value than protecting intellectual property. At the same time, to mitigate risk, the captive center set up small projects with additional vendors to enhance the learning and improve its skills. In these projects, employees' engagement at various levels and scope has helped to ensure that the captive center offers learning avenues to its staff.

> *Key motives*   Gain access to talent and capabilities; improve product and solution offering
> *Challenges*   Sourcing capabilities; demotivated staff; safeguarding intellectual property
> *Solutions*   Develop trust; ensure employee engagement; work with multiple vendors

## Conclusion

GlobalSoftware set up a basic captive unit through an acquisition in India in 1998. The basic captive unit evolved into two different hybrid models to accommodate growth. The company first developed a hybrid insourcing model in order to gain access to the necessary talent pool, react to software business cycles, and increase its access to external consultants. During the next phase of growth, the center turned toward a hybrid outsourcing model to outsource parts of the business operation and services that required either low input or seasonal skills. This allowed GlobalSoftware to achieve lower costs and greater flexibility in its processes.

# 6 From Basic to Shared: The Case of ITConsulting

Companies normally turn their captive units into shared captive centers for growth purposes. In order to develop a successful shared captive, the basic captive has to develop certain abilities to attract external clients. Some parent companies consider the shared captive model a preliminary step to a subsequent divesture. This case illustrates the range of options available to the parent firm in this regard.

## Evolving into a Shared Captive

ITConsulting, an international computer and consulting firm, decided to set up a captive center to support the four business functions of its global corporation in Hungary: human resources, financial services, accounts payable, and procurement. With its highly qualified and multilingual task teams, the captive center handled mainly back office and call center services for all global operations of the parent company. Eventually the captive center evolved to offer similar and additional services to external clients (figure 6.1). This case study focuses on the procurement function of the captive center, which currently handles the demands of both internal and external global customers.

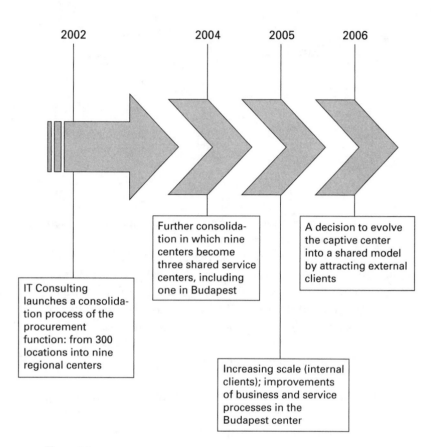

**Figure 6.1**
ITConsulting's evolution from basic to shared captive model

## Basic Captive

In 2003, ITConsulting set up three global procurement centers, integrating the processes of over three hundred different internal company locations. These global procurement operations were split into direct and indirect procurement activities. Direct procurement encompasses all items that are related to upstream procurement such as raw material, components, and parts. Indirect procurement involves dealing with suppliers regarding all other supplies and resources necessary for daily operations, including office supplies, equipment and machines, mobile phones, and rental cars. This category was subdivided into sourcing and administrative tasks. Sourcing refers to dealing with suppliers directly, a task that continued to be handled by the local offices during the initial phases of the project, while purely administrative tasks were performed by the captive center. The Hungary center was initially set up with 1,400 staff members, 280 of whom served indirect procurement functions.

With respect to the underlying strategy for establishing the captive center, the BTO procurement manager stated, "We [were] one of the first five companies in the world with such an end-to-end process from a procurement standpoint, as well as HR. We are the experts in this field. Who shall we turn to when we decide to change our business model?" ITConsulting decided to reorganize its procurement function based on its own experience and by developing a change program. It chose Hungary as the base for the procurement services because the country offered a labor pool with the necessary skills and qualifications, a rich cultural background, and stable and attractive economic and political conditions. Cost savings was another element in this decision:

"Of course, there is the reducing-costs factor as part of this decision," recalled one senior manager.

Not everything went smoothly during this change program. The dispersed procurement function and its employees were concerned that centralizing the procurement function would cause some of them to lose their jobs. The impact mainly fell on the transfer of knowledge and the degree of collaboration between the dispersed functions and the new location of the captive center. The captive center in Hungary also needed to deal with some language barriers, high attrition levels, and the challenge to staff key positions within the captive center quickly.

There was also resistance to change from some of the internal clients, as users had been following certain procedures for ten to fifteen years. Indeed, the newly established captive center managed to recruit a young and fresh generation of skilled employees who were enthusiastic about developing new ideas and exploring new ways of performing the procurement function. This also presented a different set of challenges to the captive center's top team: retaining the experts in a heated market while allowing those who were less willing to change to leave the captive center.

The change program presented cultural challenges as well. The degree of coordination and the centralization of the procurement function in Hungary shifted the power relations between the different dispersed functions into the captive center. Not everyone was comfortable with this change, and since much of the change occurred without meeting face to face, some cultural clashes emerged. One senior manager explained, "You would face debates and clashes in such situation, in particular when things are managed over conference calls and meetings, and sometimes the feeling was that we needed to create our role and protect it."

The captive unit grew rapidly during its first year. The growth rate has stabilized since then, and the focus of the captive center has shifted from growth activities to providing services in the area of administrative tasks. In consideration of the strong service capabilities developed by the captive center, the top team requested that the captive center also take on the sourcing procurement function. Such a development would have allowed the captive center to move up the value chain and expand its clientele base. However, the parent firm was reluctant to shift additional work to the center.

The captive center took advantage of this pause in its development to strengthen some critical business processes. It has established a routine communication protocol with its internal clients, as well as with the dispersed procurement functions, to ensure smooth service delivery and the continuous acquisition of knowledge during the transition phase. The captive center also relocated staff from the dispersed procurement function to closely work with the captive center staff during transition. These two change management processes rapidly ramped up the skills base of the captive center employees and enabled them to improve services in the area of administrative sourcing.

Gradually the captive center extended its internal clientele base for administrative sourcing and acquired experience in the area of sourcing in general. Its top team decided that instead of attempting to shift general sourcing (direct and indirect) work to the captive center, they should venture out and seek to extend the clientele base by attracting external clients. For this to happen, the captive center needed to coordinate this development with the parent firm.

Basic

---

*Key motives*   Save costs; centralize processes
*Challenges*   Retain knowledge; address language and cultural problems
*Solutions*   Ramp up domain knowledge; develop new markets

---

## Shared Captive

Two and a half years after establishing the Hungarian captive center and following the approach developed by its top team, the parent firm decided "the competitive advantage of Hungary in terms of knowledge and costs could allow them to start talking to external clients and selling services," recalled one senior manager. A determining factor in the decision to approach external clients was that "you have to build up the knowledge and you have to be confident that your people can serve the internal client first, and when the unit matures to a certain level of experience, you can [then] put these people in front of the [external] client." Furthermore, the parent firm's size (more than 330,000 people) and global scope were necessary to minimize the possibility that competitors could develop similar capabilities within the captive center. One manager explained: "Of course, you can understand and learn how our tools work, but not so many companies can utilize the power offered by [ITConsulting]."

As part of the preparations to evolve into a shared captive center, the team set up satellite centers close to its three global procurement centers. These centers attracted clients needing administrative outsourcing services. The senior center manager explained, "What we have done during the last couple of years, we move more and more into the sourcing part. . . . We did that to move up the value chain and to start supporting external clients as well." This decision to set up the satellite centers helped the captive center to develop the shared captive model further, as contacts with the other centers providing direct procurement services offered opportunities for the captive center to develop new business. Revenues have steadily grown, and new customers perceive their engagement with ITConsulting as a one-stop shop that provides them with a full range of procurement services.

As the captive center expanded its clientele base, the parent firm examined the services provided internally to assess the impact on its own service level agreements (SLAs). This examination revealed the parent firm was not negatively affected by the expansion. The internal client base continued to generate 70 percent of the work, and the captive center continued to devote sufficient attention to the parent firm's needs. Furthermore, only 70 of the 280 procurement staff handled external clients, further evidence of the parent firm–centric approach that the shared captive center used.

The move from basic to shared captive center offered some learning avenues to the captive center and the parent firm. First, the parent firm had to obtain the necessary government permits to sell services to local and international clients. Then the captive center needed to strategize a way to attract global customers, something it had never done before. One senior manager described the daily reality: "There [were some] deals we lost because these clients just wanted to come and learn how to do it, which is not a problem; we do [that] ourselves. Other clients were more attracted by other centers, which were cheaper. Of course, you compete in the market, and sometimes it is very difficult to get clients on board." It was a sharp learning curve for the captive center that marketing and sales were not part of its capability menu. As an immediate reaction, the captive center dropped its service fees to ensure that it could start competing on price.

Once the captive center started servicing external clients, it also had to learn how to manage those relationships. The senior procurement manager recalled: "It was a pain, dealing with a client. Of course, for our people and for the management, this resulted in . . . more workload . . . more stress, more executive attention on everything, which sometimes didn't help the business to grow smoothly." The captive center had to find ways to meet specific clients' needs because clients expected to be serviced based on their unique circumstances: "We have clients with language specifics, different working days, and different working hours."

Finally, the captive center had to adapt its business strategy to deal with the long time frame associated with negotiating contracts, which needed to include all necessary terms and conditions. Because the captive center had previously dealt only with internal clients, this drawn-out contract process was a bit of a shock for team members.

Clearly the captive center needed to attract global customers while building up credentials with existing clients and improving the quality of the service. While focusing on service improvements, the captive center took advantage of the parent firm's immense global network and its engagements with potential clients. Therefore, the approach to develop the clientele base in this case was subject to the parent firm's willingness to offer the captive center business leads. As the links with the parent firm tightened, the captive center also reshaped some of the internal procedures, in particular with regard to addressing specific client needs. The Business Transactions Outsourcing (BTO) procurement manager recalled the new approach: "Before we say we can do it [for the client], we have to make sure we could support such a request, something we did not bother to think about in the past." For this reason, communication channels in the form of regular meetings and reports were set up between the service unit and the business managers of the captive center to ensure expectations were communicated in line with the captive center's ability to support any promises made.

Pricing was another area of the business that went through changes. A flexible pricing model was developed to support the various situations the captive center faced with regard to client needs and competitors' pricing strategies. However, pricing continued to be a challenge for the Hungarian captive center, as competition came from lower-cost countries or countries with more flexibility built into their business models. Therefore, nearly every bid required top management to go back to the captive center pricing model and reexamine it, looking for additional sources of cost reductions.

Basic      Shared

> *Key motives*   Increase revenues; move up the value chain
> *Challenges*   Government requirements; attracting customers;
> price setting; contract management and monitoring
> *Solutions*   Access parent firm's network; introduce flexible
> pricing model; study competition; continue improving services; work with the local government

## Conclusion

ITConsulting set up an international basic captive center in Hungary to support its global procurement needs. Initially the center handled mostly back office and call center services for all global operations of the parent company. Eventually as the captive center's capabilities and knowledge grew, the center evolved, expanding its services to external clients around the globe. Through its expansion into a shared captive center, ITConsulting increased its revenues and moved up the parent company's value chain, gaining valuable domain knowledge, developing a greater business culture mind-set, and developing its own sales and marketing knowledge and skills set.

# 7 Divesting the Captive Center: The Case of GlobalAirline

Our research revealed three types of captive center divestures: private equity, vendor/business process outsourcing (BPO) service provider, and joint venture agreement. In essence, the act of divesture in each of these models leads to the same result: the sale of part or all of the captive center. The process through which the sale happens is different in each case. This chapter examines the divestiture of the captive center to a private equity firm.

## Evolving into a Shared, Divested Captive

As a former captive center of GlobalAirline (the parent firm), an international airline company, GlobalOutsourcer provides offshoring process services to the insurance, banking, travel, manufacturing, retail, logistics, and utilities sectors, among others. Service offerings include processes such as passenger revenue accounting, health claims processing, and end-to-end auto claims handling, to name just a few.

The basic captive center was initially set up as a wholly owned subsidiary in 1996. Just a few months later, it began offering services to external clients. Finally, it was sold to a private equity in 2002. Since then, the former captive center has expanded its services worldwide while maintaining its primary operations in India. In 2006, it entered the stock market as a publicly traded entity. A customer base of over 250 clients worldwide led to revenues of approximately $400 million in 2009. The company has now grown to more than eighteen thousand employees globally. During and after its spin-off, the captive center acquired many other companies in the insurance and travel industry in order to further expand its scope and service offerings. (See figure 7.1.)

**Basic Captive**

In 1996, the former management director of GlobalAirline noticed that "if [the parent firm] wants to survive, it has to get itself into much better shape." The senior general manager of the engineering department was assigned the task of analyzing potential cost savings of around 2 billion pounds sterling. He focused on passenger revenue accounting and "identified that [it] could be the ideal opportunity to move high-volume but low-skilled work offshore." Over six hundred GlobalAirline staff were fully dedicated to this business unit. Although GlobalAirline was very familiar with outsourcing parts of services to third parties, it did not outsource passenger revenue accounting because it viewed this activity as the lifeblood of the organization. Therefore, maintaining control of this process was essential to the company strategy and its mind-set.

In August 1996, GlobalAirline opted to create a wholly owned captive center in India, which brought down costs while maintaining process control. The captive center was run as an independent profit center to ensure positive returns for the airline. GlobalAirline chose India as the best start-up country because it had direct flights from its headquarters to

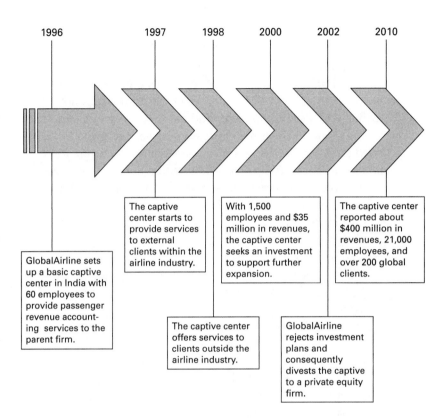

**Figure 7.1**
GlobalAirline's evolution from basic captive into a divested captive model

India; moreover, an internal infrastructure was already in place, which allowed an easier transfer of data and information. Furthermore, the captive center did not face any of the normal culture problems because knowledge about the market and habits was already available in-house. GlobalAirline was also impressed by Indian workers' proficiency with the English. The Indian government was receptive and offered large tax breaks and other benefits to the airline for establishing its captive center facility within the country. The captive center was set up under a subdivision of the airline and was eventually responsible for providing services and systems developed at the parent company to other airlines and customers.

The company sent a general manager experienced in customer service, sales, and marketing in foreign countries to set up the captive center. Almost immediately after it began operations, the captive center took on processes beyond passenger revenue accounting services, such as customer relations. "Again, this was a high-volume activity, requiring a very quick turnaround. The prime reason for moving in[to] that area was that it was becoming very expensive as a department to run. It meant extra staff, and that became a head count problem for [the parent company]," recalled one senior manager. Therefore, moving activities that had high volumes but required low-skilled employees to cut costs was the prime motivator behind establishing a captive center and expanding the service base in India.

Since the airline was already active in the country and the captive center's staff identified themselves as employees of the captive center and not GlobalAirline (to prevent union problems), the captive center was not named after the parent company and was set up instead as a wholly owned subsidiary. Another major positive effect of being a separately named entity was the flexibility the center gained with respect to growth potential. As the former general manager points out, "It became easier for me to be able to trade. If I would have been a captive center with the name of the parent company, there would have been major restrictions."

Clearly GlobalAirline's main expectation for the captive center was cost reduction. The cost of staff in India offered about 80 percent cost savings as compared to the cost of staff in the airline's home country, one source estimated. However, as the former general manager explained, "[Although] we were going to be able to save costs in various areas, the cost savings will not be seen through the first year." There were costs associated with training programs, recruitment efforts, and set-up expenditures that eroded the promise of immediate cost savings. "There is no way that before nine months to a year, those head-cost savings start to move through and show up at the bottom line," continued the former general manager. The disappointment on the parent firm's side hampered the relationship between the captive center and the parent firm, a contributing factor to the parent firm's decision to divest the captive later.

There were also challenges with integrating the captive center into the airline's global strategy. Some parts of the airline expressed discomfort with the idea that the offshore captive center was growing quickly while the source of the business came from transactions performed onshore. From time to time, the captive center's top team faced resistance from established units of the airline that refused to commit additional business to the center. However, driven by the airline's cost-cutting agenda, headquarters continued to support the shift of work to the offshore captive center, realizing that this was the only way to achieve significant savings.

At the same time, the refusal of some business units to off-shore their work drove the captive center to seek other revenue sources, some of which were eventually external clients.

Dealing with the unions was another area of experimentation for the captive center and parent firm. The parent firm eventually took the approach that the unions should be incorporated into the decision-making process regarding off-shored work, especially because the unions were a strong and influential presence in GlobalAirline's home country. Initially the unions were concerned that jobs would get lost to India and that India's working conditions were below the home country standards, but since the unions operated from onshore, their exposure to the work conditions in India was rather limited.

Although the anticipated cost savings did not materialize immediately, the captive center managed to avoid some of the problems common to young captive centers in India. First, the center managed to maintain low attrition levels, a result of fair payment and attractive career paths. The center also grew quickly because of the airline's hiring freeze, which eventually drove many of the business units to offshore work to the captive center. This was done despite the resentment expressed by onshore staff about the role that the captive center had taken within the firm. Nevertheless, onshore staff soon realized that "it was a huge advantage to get away from all that rubbish work they had to do, which was important work that had to be done, but it was at a very low-skilled level," one senior manager explained. The parent firm also benefited from the 24/7 work regime instituted by the captive center, which "enabled the captive center and the parent firm to cut the turnaround time to our customer, [GlobalAirline], dramatically."

After stability emerged, additional benefits for both parent firm and captive center became clear. The captive center was able to outsource some low-level tasks to local vendors, further improving its cost base. As the captive center matured, the parent firm internally regulated the offshoring processes, guiding all business units to use its offshore asset. Gradually the resistance to the captive center faded away.

To secure a smooth setup of its Indian captive center and prevent any problems with the unions, the parent firm established a program in which union representatives were regularly updated. Some union representatives were even sent to India to see the captive center and learn about the working conditions there. The captive center benefited from this new, close relationship with the unions because some practices applied onshore were introduced in the captive center. These developments helped the captive center recruit and retain the necessary talent.

Basic

> *Key motives*   Cost savings; develop a 24/7 work regime; free up staff in the home country; leverage the brand image of the parent company
> *Challenges*   Setting up challenges, allocating growth opportunities; working closely with the parent firm; overcoming onshore staff and union resistance
> *Solutions*   Create partnership with the parent firm; integrate unions into the offshoring process; make the captive center's value visible to the entire firm

## Shared Captive

The captive center began operations in 1996 with fifty to sixty staff members in an office with the capacity of three hundred employees. The former general manager recalled: "We got an advantage here, and I had a number of companies coming to me to ask what [GlobalAirline] was up to and what was going on. I realized that we had a commercial advantage. The advantage was the brand name of [GlobalAirline], and that we were one of the very few organizations in India that had the capacity to take on work from outside. So I started to offer the captive center's services [and] commercial opportunities to other airlines."

Over time the captive center became known for providing specialist computer skills in areas such as ticketing and computer-based training. External clients started to pay attention to the services offered by the captive center, realizing they could benefit from the expertise and services the unit had developed. The parent firm opened additional marketing channels, mainly through the worldwide alliance programs it had set up with other airlines. Therefore, it was logical for the captive center to start trading with members of this alliance. The concern of losing important information to competitors was not a critical factor, commented one senior manager, as "the information would be of no use to [GlobalAirline] or to anybody else. It was post-flight work. [Airlines] are more secretive about their marketing. What we were offering had nothing to do with marketing." Additionally, security and confidentiality clauses structured in contracts ensured the staff would not disseminate specific or proprietary information about the airline. Finally, that the captive center did not have the name of the parent company elevated the trust level of potential clients within the airline industry.

By November 1996, the captive center had gained three external clients. Financially, it was expected to break even in 1998. However, before the center could expand its service offerings to external clients, the general manager had to obtain permission from the parent firm. This manager developed a business case for the expansion plan and presented it to the parent firm's board. On this occasion, the board quickly approved the plan. In particular, the board was attracted by the fact that the captive center "was able to sell services, which will bring down the unit cost back to [GlobalAirline]," recalled one senior manager. In 1998, the captive center began offering its services to clients that were outside the airline industry, such as companies in the insurance industry. This opportunity to penetrate the insurance industry arose through the parent firm's network. One of the management directors of the parent firm was also on the executive board of an interested insurance company, and he made the introduction. By 2000, the captive unit was providing services to more than nine other airlines and had annual revenues of $25 million.[1]

The captive center faced some challenges as its growth accelerated. In particular, it had to create marketing and sales channels as well as meet specific customer demand, all while restructuring to accommodate external clients. In parallel, the captive center needed to ensure that services provided to the parent firm would not be compromised as a result of the expansion. Operating under a high degree of skepticism from onshore staff required the center to ensure that its first and main client was satisfied.

To strengthen the delivery model and service quality, the captive center developed a much stronger delivery capability in the form of client engagement, relationship management, and contract monitoring. It also formalized its sourcing relationships with the parent firm, supporting them with service level agreements (SLAs). The development of new services to both internal and external clients was carried out in cooperation with the parent firm in order to ensure transparency regarding the growth of the captive center, as well as to provide an option to the parent firm to purchase new services.

Basic     Shared

*Key motives*   Induce efficiencies; increase asset use; increase revenue
*Challenges*   Lack of marketing and sales capabilities; maintaining good relationships with the parent firm
*Solutions*   Improve the delivery model; leverage the relationships with the parent firm to enter new industries

### Divesting to a Private Equity Firm

In 2000, when the captive center achieved success in offering services to external clients and gradually had become regarded as a leading BPO unit in India, its top team divulged a plan to grow even further. By that time, 44 percent of its $20 million business revenue was generated through engagements with external clients. Out of fifteen hundred captive staff members, 65 percent worked on the parent firm's account, and 35 percent were dedicated to external customers. The former general manager of the captive center outlined the growth plan and sent it to the parent firm's board. "When I forwarded the five-year plan to the management director of [GlobalAirline], he said, 'What are you smoking? You put forward a plan here for twelve thousand staff, which is about 30 percent extra head count.'" The parent firm responded to the former general manager's growth plan by saying, "We are running an airline; we are not an investment house." The parent firm had other priorities and the captive center's plan to expand further was rejected. However, ongoing investments were needed to build skills "around selling BPO services, around getting confidence built, around building track records and reference cases that require a commercial engine," one senior manager recalled. A clash arose inside the management structure as well as between the management of the captive unit and its parent company. "So, it became obvious that the only way the captive center was able to advance was to be sold off," concluded the former general manager.

In 2001, the airline considered a takeover by an investor. Negotiations were based on reaching "an agreement which would allow the future growth and development of the captive center, with the airline still retaining a significant stake in the business."[2] In 2002, the parent firm sold 70 percent of its equity stake to a private equity firm.[3] The airline retained the remaining stake simply to mitigate the risk of offering its captive center's operations and services at too low a price to the private equity firm. According to an outside research expert, "They were not holding that stake to have a major management decision in the firm. They were holding it to try to make some kind of return when the value of that firm increased."

The parent firm chose to sell to a private equity firm because "money-wise, they were coming up with a good offer. But, we also felt that they had the right structure and the right culture, because one of the areas we had to deal with was to protect the interest of the airline because the airline was the principal customer," said one senior manger from GlobalAirline. As a result of the divestiture, the parent firm was able to refocus on its core businesses and start treating its former captive center as a vendor.[4] It was important to the airline that operations continued unchanged; however, the captive center gained the ability to develop business opportunities beyond the airline industry and was able to enter new geographies following investments made by the new owner.

For its part, the private equity firm was interested in acquiring the captive center because "the captive [had] already established a leading position in the business process outsourcing segment in India."[5] Furthermore, "the basis of the captive, its infrastructure, its setup, its management team, who saw the opportunity to grow the business, was very attractive to an operation. If you tried to do that from day one, it would have probably taken you a couple of years to get to the same stage." The captive center had established an excellent reputation, elevated by its ISO 9000 certification and Six Sigma model. According to the former general manager, "All it needed was massive investments."

At the time, India had a unique advantage in the BPO market due to its skilled labor pool, technological expertise, and managerial talent. The private equity firm stated during the divestiture process that "the business process outsourcing sector worldwide is poised to witness tremendous growth. Couple this with the established track record and formidable competencies, the captive center has been built as one of the first movers in the sector, and we see this as a valuable investment in building a leading global organization."[6] The CEO of the private equity firm agreed: "With this captive center, we now have deep domain knowledge of the sector and will use the company to grow organically as well as through acquisitions in the Indian BPO space."[7]

The private equity firm bought the captive unit on the condition that the contract to the parent firm, in terms of the processing work, would be retained on a commercial basis. As the captive center had been set up as an independent company "that [had] its own corporate identity and an independent charter for the growth and development of the business,"[8] the private equity firm allotted $3 million to the captive unit to establish a third center in India by 2003, which would allow it to increase staff to up to ten thousand employees in the five years following the divestiture. The new general manager for the captive center commented, "We can grow organically at 50 percent a year to the foreseeable future."

Within its first year of running as an independent company, the captive center grew by more than 120 percent, to $33.5 million in revenues.[9] Due to the rapid growth, the unit went public in July 2006. This allowed the former parent firm, as well as the private equity firm, to gain a significant return on their investment while selling off most of their remaining stake.

The captive center gradually increased its staff count to over twenty-one thousand employees (as of June 2010) and still growing. The buyout created new advantages for the employees; they became core staff members of an independent company and were no longer considered back office workers. After the divestiture, the captive center was able to attract better talent.

Rapid growth was possible because the private equity firm recognized the need to invest several million dollars to help the organization grow in order to rebuild the communication infrastructure, bring in some senior management, and use their contacts and their networking. Hence, the captive center had the opportunity to fully explore its range of assets and possibilities. Although 40 percent of revenue still comes from the travel industry, the strongest segment of the captive center, banking, financial services, and insurance together account for another 40 percent of revenue. The emerging segments of manufacturing, retail and consumer products have increased to 20 percent.[10]

Arjun Sethi, principal manager of A.T. Kearney, notes that the captive center "has carved out an attractive niche for itself in servicing the airline and healthcare sector. The competition is relatively moderated, as is the availability of skills for such work."[11] According to the director for investments and alliances of the parent firm "The venture has turned out more successfully than most of the airline leadership expected. There was no question that the airline made the right decision. The company has benefited from both its initial stake in what became a successful commercial venture and the fact that its business processes are being done by a more efficient and viable entity."

There were some concerns throughout the divestment process—in particular, from the parent firm. For one, the due diligence and agreement with the private equity firm lasted over eighteen months, during which there were concerns that service levels and attrition rates would deteriorate because of uncertainty regarding the future of the captive center. As the agreement was formed, the parent firm also sought to secure the positions of some key personnel within the captive center to ensure the continuity of the service and relationships it held with the parent firm. Finally, as the BPO market became crowded in India, the captive center had to find a way to "retain its identity and market position, especially when larger multinational players such as IBM have entered the Indian market with an acquisitive eye."[12] The captive center had to start fighting for contracts, which required it to strengthen its sales and marketing capabilities even more.

Step by step, the captive center built its delivery capabilities under private equity ownership. To ensure the service level provided to the parent firm remained unaffected, over one hundred new SLAs were put in place between the airline and the captive center. Although the parent firm was concerned over losing key employees, it also recognized that the business objectives of the captive center were bound to change, and as a result, changes in personnel had to be expected.

Basic   Shared   Divested private equity

*Key motives*   Focus on the parent firm's core activities; allow the captive center to grow through investments made by a third party.
*Challenges*   Retaining morale during negotiations; understanding the objectives of the buying party; protecting the service after the spin-off
*Solutions*   Introduce service contracts between captive center and parent firm; seek growth through investments

**Conclusion**

GlobalAirline initially set up its Indian captive center as a
wholly owned subsidiary in 1996, providing passenger
revenue accounting for the parent company. Almost immediately, the captive center evolved into a shared business
unit providing limited services to a few third-party clients.
As its external market grew, GlobalAirline sold the shared
captive center to a private equity firm in 2002 in order to
expand its services globally throughout multiple industries.
It was only through divestiture that the captive center was
able to fully realize and capitalize on its domain expertise
and capacity for growth.

# 8 Divesting the Captive Center: The Case of AmeriBank

In the previous chapter, we looked at the acquisition of a captive center by a private equity firm. This section examines the acquisition of the AmeriBank captive center by a business process outsourcing (BPO) service provider.

## Evolving into a Divested Captive

The former captive center of AmeriBank, one of the world's largest financial services banks, was set up through a strategic acquisition in 1992 for handling security and leasing operations. In 1999 AmeriBank restructured the captive center into a publicly traded BPO responsible for corporate and consumer banking. The captive center managed customer call centers, document imaging, and information technology (IT) support for AmeriBank's various global entities and employed 12,500 in seven Indian locations.[1] In October 2008, AmeriBank divested its captive BPO to IndiaIT, a leading Indian BPO company.

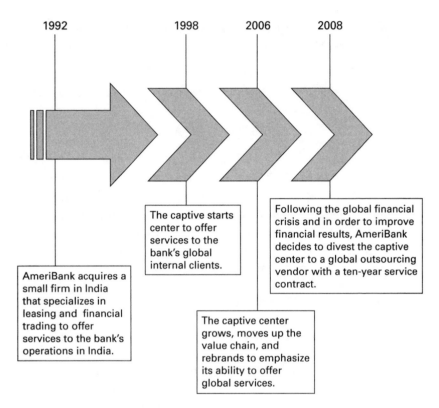

**Figure 8.1**
AmeriBank's evolution from basic captive center into a divested captive model

## Basic Captive

In 1992 AmeriBank took over an existing company that provided security, leasing, and financial trading activities for its corporations in India. The head of operations explained the reasons for the acquisition: "It had to do with a lot of regulations on brokerage and security trading during that time. So, AmeriBank decided to take an existing company which had all those licenses. It helped [AmeriBank] to get an entry into the brokerage business in India."

In 1998 AmeriBank began transforming its Indian captive center into a global BPO unit that provided corporate banking solutions for the bank's global units, including cash management, trade finance, and credit cards. AmeriBank decided to offshore these activities to its captive center due to confidentiality reasons, large transaction sizes, and the level of complexity in these processes. "Within corporate banking operations, there was also the nature of the transaction involving a large amount of money and the complexity of the transactions, which [AmeriBank], at that time, felt would be better done by an in-house company," explained one senior manager. Other important advantages for AmeriBank were certain cost advantages and the time zone differences, which allowed 24/7 operations. In addition, India's skilled labor pool ensured that the captive center could ramp up operations if needed.

The captive center aggressively sought to pursue a commercial approach. The head of operations recalled that the captive center "pitched almost like a third-party provider, negotiated rates and responded to Request for Proposals." Taking on global operations also helped improve processes across the parent firm. Gradually the captive center assumed additional service lines and extended its offering to the parent firm's business units across the globe. In 2006 the company "moved up the value chain by executing complex processes in cash management and mortgages, and with risk analytics and global management service line portfolio[s]."[2] This was possible because the captive center had proven itself to the parent firm, and satisfactory ratings allowed it to increase its level of control and compliance.

In late 2006 the captive center changed its name to AmeriBank Global Services (AGS).[3] According to AmeriBank's CEO and managing director, "The name emphasizes the geographic spread and diversity of our customers in AmeriBank, and the wide range of products and services that we offer. For all of us, it reflects a closer association and synchronous identity with our parent company." The name change further enhanced the captive's capabilities, enabling the captive center to attract additional internal customers and grow organically. The captive center was ranked among the top 100 largest Indian companies in terms of sales.

This growth path was not free of challenges. As the captive grew, it aimed at reducing its dependence on the parent firm and sought to focus on non-AmeriBank customers. However, AmeriBank rejected the captive's growth plan and restricted it to holding the parent company as its only customer.

The captive center also faced wage inflation issues, which were in the range of 15 to 20 percent annually, and annual attrition levels continued to remain high, at 25 to 40 percent. The units that required advanced language skills and were performing shifts to provide services to U.S. clients faced the highest attrition rate, as staff with advanced language skills were in demand, and those who performed shifts sought positions with better conditions and a more promising career path. A 2007 press release by AGS stated, "Although we have a large talent pool, there has been growing concern about parts of the available pool being unsuitable for employment in [the] BPO industry."

In an attempt to overcome the high attrition rate, the captive center implemented its Employee First mission, which brought in different initiatives and training offerings to ensure a robust working environment and the development of employee skills and abilities. Furthermore, the captive center changed its name in 2006 to include the name of its parent firm. According to the CEO of AGS, "[AmeriBank's] brand name will also help to make the company an 'employer of choice' in an industry where employee turnover rate is very high."[4] Thereafter, the captive turnover rate decreased to 37 percent, bringing the attrition rate below that of the industry average.

To overcome the challenge of losing domain knowledge because of high attrition levels, the captive center offered comprehensive training sessions on industry-specific programs. The center also included mitigating mechanisms such as "constantly revising and revaluating the pay scale, providing people who work in the night shift with a certain extra amount of money to help them overcome that hardship, providing transport, meals, recreation facilities on site and supervisory management programs on how to manage their times," explained the head of operations.

Language problems were circumvented by not positioning activities requiring a high level of English skills, such as call center activities, in India. The head of operations recalled, "Voice-based call center activities were not a very large component of [AGS]. It was always the back office that was [the] large[st] part." Additional actions were taken to overcome the basic language problems experienced within the business units themselves: "Language problems were addressed by better training, by getting language specialists from the USA to come and work in India on site, sending our people overseas, constantly upgrading our accent neutralization programs—not necessarily trying to make our agents speak like Americans, but making sure whatever they said was clearly understood by Americans."

The parent firm also clearly realized the need for data protection and privacy, as well as security practices and processes. In 2006, it implemented recommended new anti-cybercrime legal frameworks.

Basic

---

*Key motives*   Reduce costs; centralize operations; achieve scale and gain access to knowledge and skills
*Challenges*   Attrition rate; language problems; scale and growth
*Solutions*   Training; service improvements; certification; employee development programs

---

### Divesting to a BPO Provider

In 2007 the global financial crisis hit AmeriBank along with the rest of the industry. The bank reported an annual loss of $8.3 billion in 2008 and consequently decided to restructure its business units. The restructuring plan was based on achieving a cost-cutting strategy of $2.5 billion by 2009. In addition, the company wanted to refocus its strategy to offer new services more quickly and with better cost-effectiveness. According to AmeriBank's filing with he U.S. Securities and Exchange Commission, the company planned to save $775 million in 2007 and $1.6 billion in 2008 by reducing its IT and back office operating costs. Half of the data processing centers and IT sections were set to be closed down.

This strategic move was in line with previous strategies that focused on outsourcing a number of tech functions to Indian-based vendors. The chief executive of AmeriBank stated, "Our new organizational model marks a further important step along the path we are pursuing to make AmeriBank simpler, leaner and a more efficient organization that works collaboratively across the businesses and throughout the world to benefit clients and shareholders."[5] According to the head of operations, "[AmeriBank], as a company, wanted to focus on the core business of banking. A BPO unit, while associated with banking, was not the core business of banking itself. . . . There is a greater degree of comfort with outsourcing. There is greater control, there is much better comfort regarding confidentiality."

In October 2008, AmeriBank sold its 96.3 percent stake in the Indian captive center, along with the intellectual property rights, for $505 million to IndiaIT.[6] IndiaIT expected the captive center to be fully integrated with the vendor's operations within a few months. Part of the deal included a $2.5 billion contract for nine and a half years between AmeriBank and IndiaIT, which ensured that AmeriBank would purchase the same line of services from its former captive units as before.[7] This contract allowed IndiaIT to generate 6 percent of its annual revenues from its alliance with AmeriBank.

Because AmeriBank had been a customer of IndiaIT in the area of application development, infrastructure support, help desk, and other process outsourcing services since 1992, AmeriBank executives saw IndiaIT as a good fit for the captive center and future relationships with the parent firm. AmeriBank believed its previous experiences would allow a smoother knowledge transfer and a more successful cooperative endeavor.

The divestiture to IndiaIT also brought nonfinancial advantages to AmeriBank. As the CEO of AmeriBank Asia noted, "Our customers require access to increasingly complex processing solutions, and this relationship will achieve a 'best in class' technology model that capitalizes on both [AmeriBank's] expertise in financial services and [IndiaIT's] expertise in process optimization."[8] The head of operations added: "While being a part of another company which is a larger firm, you get the advantages of scale. Some of these benefits of the economies of scale would come back to [AmeriBank] itself." From an investor viewpoint, IndiaIT was able to gain end-to-end IT and BPO services in global banking and financial services. The CEO and managing director commented on this acquisition: "This gives us a unique advantage, as these core banking operations have remained within the limit of captive organization thus far. So we can create a new market for third-party BPO and core financial services to be targeted at large global financial institutions."[9] Tejas Doshi, head of research at brokerage firm Sushil Finance in Mumbai, pointed out more advantages of the acquisition: "This deal ensures revenue visibility for [IndiaIT], since [AmeriBank] itself is a very big organization, which is a big positive in these challenging times. It is an opportunity for [IndiaIT] to get new business at a decent price."[10]

This strategic change was not completely smooth for the parties. AmeriBank benefited from the captive center's strong position, mainly because of the strong relationships it created between its business units. As the CEO of AmeriBank pointed out, this was an essential factor in its strategy: "The success of our organization lies in the strong partnership and collaboration of our people in our global businesses and geographic regions."[11] The question was whether IndiaIT and the acquired captive center could maintain a teamwork culture with the former parent firm once those relationships were based on an outsourcing contract. And as the global financial sector goes through a major shakeup, IndiaIT has reasons to be concerned that the $2.5 billion contract with AmeriBank could become invalid if the former parent firm were to be sold to another party.

But the parties involved so far have built a fruitful cooperation. There seems to be trust between the two companies, and top teams from both sides are endeavoring to make this relationship work. The CEO and managing director of IndiaIT stated, "Our acquisition, and consequently, the long-term contractual commitment, also cement this important relationship and take it a step further."[12] The head of operations of AmeriBank is not concerned that the former parent firm will get less attention after divestiture simply because of the mitigating strategies carried out by AmeriBank prior to the divestment, such as building capabilities in the United States and the magnitude of the contract.

*Key Motives*   Focus on core activities; improve financial results
*Challenges*   Finding the most appropriate buyer; setting up a contingency plan for after the divestment
*Solutions*   Due diligence with potential buyers; strengthened cooperation with the buying party; building sourcing capabilities

**Conclusion**

AGS, a former captive center of AmeriBank, one of the world's largest financial services banks, was acquired in 1992 for the purpose of handling security and leasing operations for the Indian arm of AmeriBank. In 1998 AGS extended its service offerings to the entire global organization. In October 2008 AmeriBank divested its captive unit to IndiaIT, a leading Indian BPO company. The divestiture allowed AmeriBank to refocus on core activities, and AGS developed key organizational design capabilities, increased domain expertise, and a synergy between operational knowledge and IT capabilities.

# 9  Divesting the Captive Center: The Case of ConsumerGoods

In the two preceding chapters, we examined cases of divestiture in which a private equity and a business process outsourcing (BPO) provider were involved. This chapter looks at a divestiture of a captive center in which a joint venture (JV) agreement set the stage for the change of ownership.

## Evolving into a Divested Captive

The captive unit of ConsumerGoods, a worldwide consumer products company, was founded in India in 2003. ConsumerGoods India was set up as a back office for financial and accounting work for ConsumerGoods's worldwide and Indian locations. Due to its arrangement as an independent profit center that adopted the service orientation of the parent company, the captive center was able to separate its operations from the controller department and attract internal customers, gradually becoming a more efficient enterprise.

In 2006 ConsumerGoods decided to split off all back office work it considered noncore to the company. By this time, ConsumerGoods India had achieved large-scale processing while serving internal clients. To increase its scale even

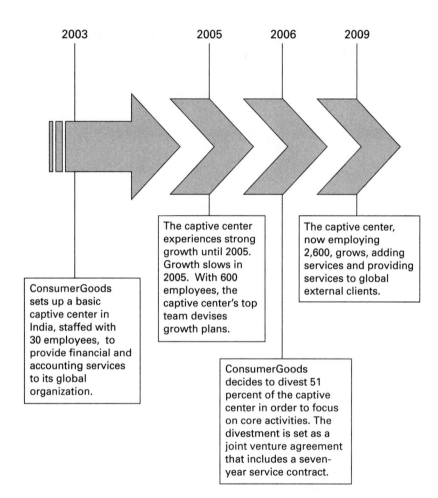

**Figure 9.1**
ConsumerGoods's evolutionary path from basic captive to divested captive model

further, it wanted to extend its services to external customers. Hence, 51 percent of the captive holding was sold in a joint venture agreement to Consulting&Outsourcing, an international operating, consulting, outsourcing, and IT company.

## Basic Captive

In 2003 ConsumerGoods established an Indian captive center to provide support functions for its finance and accounting services, which were being performed by the controller department. The parent firm felt these services should be performed in a separate unit in India and delivered with a service orientation. The head of BPO operations of Consulting&Outsourcing and former manager of ConsumerGoods India commented: "We were introducing a big change while bringing in that service mind-set into a support department. We wanted to create a service environment and gain the freedom to run the venture like entrepreneurs." Because the BPO unit had been set up as a profit center from the start, the captive center did not receive any mandates from the parent firm and had to win internal clients on its own. The center was set with three goals in mind, the head of BPO operations recalled: "First of all, it should make business sense to our customers. We had to go and sell our offerings to each country, to help them construct a business case and make it an attractive proposition. The second part was that everything had to be converted into a service mind-set. The third dimension was to liberate some of the companies from noncore activities."

To achieve these goals, two different branches were created. The first branch, consisting of twenty-five employees in Bangalore, managed ConsumerGoods's global business unit customers and provided general accounting for the factories and the headquarters, along with financial support functions on the sales side. The second branch was created with thirty staff in Chennai and was responsible for the Indian operations. India was one of the company's ten largest markets in sales; hence, this unit focused solely on Indian operations. However, both locations were operated under one banner and brand to take advantage of the ConsumerGoods reputation.

Gaining ConsumerGoods Australia as its first internal client, the captive expanded its scope quickly and started to sell its concept to various countries and various divisions of ConsumerGoods. The advantage of the Indian location was the costs arbitrage between the Indian captive centers and the business units that operated from onshore locations. The staff needed skill sets to ensure quality services at low cost while moving into an outsourcing concept.

But the parent firm and the captive center faced some challenges. Set up as a separate service entity, ConsumerGoods India had to actively sell and promote its services internally; there were no handouts from the parent company. It also had to overcome concerns by the individual country CEOs, who associated offshoring and outsourcing with some risk. The captive center faced the challenge of meeting employees' expectations in order to overcome high attrition rates in the Indian labor market. To make matters worse, salaries were inflating as the Indian BPO market increased. Compared to the other cases studied in this book, ConsumerGoods entered the Indian market rather late in the game, which made it even more difficult to cope with the effects of a heated market.

Finally, the captive center faced limited growth opportunity and scope within the ConsumerGoods organization.

The head of BPO operations stated, "Once your market gets defined and is limited, [your] growth is also limited by that." In 2005, the captive center assessed it had only one more year of growth left within the ConsumerGoods organization before its growth curve leveled out.

To overcome these challenges, the captive center focused on developing a service orientation mentality and delivery model. As a result, ConsumerGoods India changed its organizational design and developed marketing and sales channels to enhance its viability. Going from a subunit of the controller to a BPO unit, the company quickly adapted its organizational design to address this new level of independence.

To address staffing challenges, the captive center targeted staff whose expectations could be met and who were capable of adapting to the new requirements. The captive center tried to offer career paths, realizing that this was one of the key factors in reducing attrition levels.

Basic

*Key motives*  Centralize a business function; create a service-oriented financial unit; reduce costs
*Challenges*  High attrition levels; ability to attract customers; inability to grow within its organization
*Solutions*  Invest in training; offer career paths; design and implement a service-oriented business unit

### Divesting through a Joint Venture Agreement

In 2005 ConsumerGoods India realized it had exhausted most of the growth engines available within the parent firm. At the same time, its top team sought to pursue an even more ambitious growth strategy. The head of BPO operations recalled: "[ConsumerGoods] was very clear that anything that was not core for its business will not be kept in the tent. Its business is all about marketing, creating brands, and selling them to consumers. It wanted mainly to focus on that and hence, it wanted to clearly outsource all of those [noncore] activities to any global company."

In October 2006 ConsumerGoods sold 51 percent of its captive center stake to Consulting&Outsourcing in a joint venture agreement. ConsumerGoods chose this method of divestiture to maintain control over the processes provided to the company and to ensure services continued to be performed for the parent firm. According to one senior manager from the captive center, "It had nothing to do with profits. It [had] more to do with running a particular service in the manner [ConsumerGoods] wanted it to."

Though it was obvious that the captive center needed an investment in order to grow, the parent firm decided in favor of an IT and BPO vendor simply because the buyer was "a global player that can offer scale compared to a private equity that could mainly offer capital." Consulting&Outsourcing managed operations globally and offered the captive center the scale it needed, along with additional domain knowledge. Conversely, ConsumerGoods offered Consulting&Outsourcing a platform on which to enter the Indian BPO market for finance and accounting.

As part of the JV agreement, ConsumerGoods set up a seven-year contract with Consulting&Outsourcing to guarantee uninterrupted service. At the same time, ConsumerGoods India grew to offer services to third-party clients. During 2008, less than 50 percent of the work performed by the former captive center was for the former parent company; the rest was allocated to new external clients. Furthermore, ConsumerGoods India grew from six hundred employees at the time of divestiture to over twenty-five hundred in 2009. On March 29, 2010, Consulting&Outsourcing announced that it bought the remaining 49 percent in the captive center. Financial terms of the deal were not disclosed.

Basic    Divested through JV

*Key motives* Increasing scale and profit; focus on core activities
*Challenges faced by the captive center/parent firm* Selecting the most suitable buyer; designing a contingency plan for the day after
*Solutions applied by the captive center/parent firm* Assessment of future needs; devise a partnership solution while maintain ownership

### Conclusion

ConsumerGoods India, established in 2003, was initially set up as a back office for financial and accounting work for ConsumerGoods's worldwide and Indian locations. It was arranged as an independent profit center and maintained separate operations from the controller department. Its goal was to attract internal customers from the ConsumerGoods global network, becoming a more efficient enterprise. In 2006 ConsumerGoods decided to sell off 51 percent of its captive holding in a joint venture agreement to Consulting&Outsourcing, an international operating, consulting, outsourcing, and IT company. This divestiture through a joint venture agreement allowed ConsumerGoods to maintain control over the services the former captive entity offered, allowed ConsumerGoods India to expand into a multiclient global service provider, and gave Consulting&Outsourcing a broader service offering for its clients and gain a foothold in the Indian BPO market. The JV agreement was a win-win solution for all parties.

# 10 Migrating the Captive Center: The Case of InfoTech

This chapter presents the case of a migrated captive center owned by a leading information technology corporation (InfoTech). The chapter is structured chronologically, and the historic development of InfoTech's procurement is outlined to provide context for the eventual migration. The chapter then explains the migration of the captive center functions in detail.

## Background

Prior to 2002, procurement for InfoTech was fulfilled separately by each individual country organization, with some overreaching coordination by global councils. The procurement encompassed all processes related to buying, from the company's regular purchases to the exceptional expenses on project work. Roughly eight hundred people in more than three hundred locations were responsible for the operational tasks of procurement alone: purchase order processing, call centers, and administrative support. In order to optimize processes, InfoTech launched a corporate project in 2002 to consolidate this operational, lower-value portion of the procurement function into nine regional centers around the globe.[1] At the same time, the countries were supposed to focus on the suppliers at the marketplace and their relationships with those suppliers.

In 2004 the consolidation process intensified. The nine remaining centers were consolidated into three offshore captive centers referred to as procurement shared service centers (PSSCs): Bangalore, Shanghai, and Budapest.[2] Although organizational efficiency had been the key argument for the move in 2002, the 2004 decision to consolidate and offshore was clearly based on cost of operations: "Moving work from high-cost to low-cost countries offered a good business [solution]," the head of the center in Budapest recalls.

The original mission of these three new centers was to continue handling the internal operational, lower-added-value procurement tasks. One manager described the duties initially assigned to Budapest as "the copy-paste work they didn't like." However, as the centers proved increasingly experienced and skilled, they were given more autonomy. Consequently they expanded their scope toward more complex sourcing activities and moved up the value chain to some extent. In 2006 this strategy expanded further. The global procurement management team, the highest authority of procurement within the company, decided that each of the three procurement centers would set up its own satellite center: Vietnam for Bangalore, Chengdu for Shanghai, and Sofia for Budapest. The satellite centers would perform the lower-value operational tasks, while the three existing centers focused on the value-added and sourcing tasks they had taken over from the country organizations. Figure 10.1 summarizes the background of the InfoTech migration case.

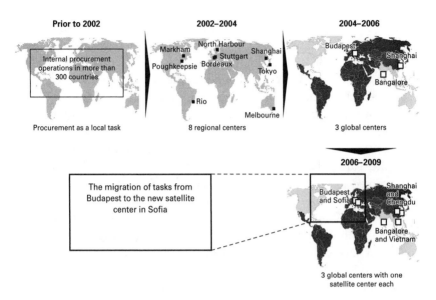

**Figure 10.1**
InfoTech historical summary

## Goals of the Migration

The outsourcing that occurred in 2002 was meant to optimize processes, whereas the consolidation of 2004 occurred due to cost considerations. While several reasons have been given for the 2006 migration of lower-value tasks from Budapest to Sofia, cost savings was seen as the most important reason. Budapest was chosen as a site location in 2004 because it was a relatively low-cost location, but since that time, Hungary had faced rapid inflation. Accordingly, it was no longer considered a low-cost country by InfoTech standards, but somewhere in the middle cost range. Bulgaria, in contrast, was considerably cheaper, by roughly 40 percent.

The second factor prompting the migration was the search for higher-value work, commented the Budapest business controls (BBC) manager: "We grew the capabilities and skills so much that we needed more value-added work. So we needed something, someone, some *place* where we could move the actual administrative work to, so we can get more value work from the country. And that's why the satellite centers were created, to free capacity to move Budapest up the value chain." People in Budapest were not only perceived as experienced and skilled enough to overtake new value-added activities, but they were bored with their old tasks, and management was concerned that talented employees would soon leave the company, leading to higher attrition levels. Management decided it would be difficult to keep both low- and high-value-added activities with different wage levels in one place, so a migration to a new captive center for some activities would need to be carried out to mitigate the problem.

**Scope of the Migration**

The logic of the migration was clear: lower-value job roles were migrated from Budapest to Sofia, and Budapest took over higher-value roles from the country organizations. The implications for the captive unit (the scope of the move) are presented in figure 10.2.

Budapest provided eight main functions when the migration began: operations, procurement contact center (PCC), procurement application support center (PASC), business transactions outsourcing (BTO), business controls, sourcing hub, systems, and SPRINT. oOperations, PCC, and PASC represented the lower-value functions of the Budapest center.

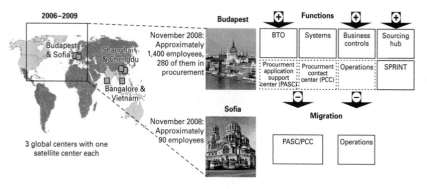

**Figure 10.2**
Migrated functions of the InfoTech captive unit

Operations processed all buying orders from the country organizations. Accordingly, the unit was subdivided by country in teams for U.K./Ireland, the Nordic countries, Central Europe, France Benelux, and Italy/Spain/Latin America. PCC was a call center function that supported internal clients with procurement problems, and PASC supported the supplier side when difficulties arose. These three lower-value tasks were the targets of the migration from Budapest to Sofia.

Conversely, BTO, business controls, and sourcing hub functions embodied the higher-value functions migrated into the Budapest center from the country organizational units. Within the newly migrated BTO division, InfoTech incorporated the entire procurement process for external, as opposed to internal, customers. The business controls division ensured the quality and stability of all processes related to procurement. The sourcing hub was the link between the sourcing activities in the country organizations (e.g., building personal relationships with the suppliers) and the more administrative work performed in the Budapest center.

These three high-value functions increasingly shifted from the country organizations to the Budapest center.

The systems and SPRINT functions were not directly affected by the migration. The former was responsible for the reporting related to procurement, and the latter mainly addressed project management tasks.

## The Migration Process

Three distinctive phases can be identified within the migration process from Budapest to Sofia (figure 10.3). In phase 1 (July 2006–February 2007), the new satellite center in Sofia needed to be established. A suitable location had to be selected and staffed with approximately thirty employees.

Phase 2 was launched once the initial team was in place and regular operations began in March 2007. Through spring 2008, the migration of tasks from Budapest to Sofia was conducted in a gradual, reactive manner. Whenever an employee in Budapest with a lower-value job role voluntarily decided to leave InfoTech or move to a higher-value job function

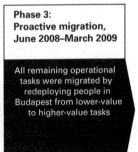

**Phase 1:**
**Setting up the Sofia center,**
**July 2006–February 2007**

Decide on location and facility; initiate recruitment; start operations

**Phase 2:**
**Reactive migration,**
**March 2007–May 2008**

From the time Sofia is fully operating, jobs roles are migrated from Hungary to Bulgaria whenever someone voluntarily leaves InfoTech Budapest or changes from a low-value to a higher-value position

**Phase 3:**
**Proactive migration,**
**June 2008–March 2009**

All remaining operational tasks were migrated by redeploying people in Budapest from lower-value to higher-value tasks

**Figure 10.3**
Phases of migration

within the firm, his or her former role was not restaffed in Budapest but moved to Sofia instead. In this way, the company did not suffer attrition through worries of job loss, but instead used naturally occurring attrition to migrate jobs and tasks to the new center in Sofia.

In phase 3, which began in June 2008, management decided to accelerate the migration: instead of waiting for employees to leave lower-value operational tasks of their own accord, they promoted redeployment of staff to higher-value roles in Budapest. Naturally occurring attrition was not working; the company needed to stimulate the process in order to fully migrate all remaining lower-value tasks to Sofia by March 2009.

### Phase 1: Setting Up the Sofia Center

Once the decision had been made to establish a satellite center for Budapest, the global procurement management had to find a suitable location and start operations from scratch. They set January 2007 as the deadline by which the center was to be fully staffed and operational.

In early summer 2006, a team from the corporate center assessed suitable locations based on multiple criteria: cost; infrastructure; maturity of the local InfoTech organization; and macroeconomic data such as unemployment, number of universities and their location, number of university graduates, languages spoken, business skills, government support, and level of "overheating" of the labor market. As characterized by the Sofia center manager, "Everything you can think of was included." InfoTech's assessment process was rigorous and comprehensive.

Although there was no clear agreement about which countries and cities should be incorporated into the research assessment, both Romania (one or two cities other than

Bucharest) and Bulgaria (Sofia) were short-listed as potential sites. Two vice presidents, one from operations and one from sourcing, were involved in this evaluation process and visited both candidate countries.[3]

In September 2006, only four months before the center was scheduled to be fully operational, Romania appeared the likely choice: "In September, it was 99 percent agreed that this satellite location would be in Romania," the global business controls (GBC) manager stated. Human resources for the local InfoTech country organization, along with other external agencies, began screening the Romanian market for potential employees. However, the study groups ultimately discarded the Romanian option in favor of Sofia. The head of the center and the Sofia center manager believed the main factor in the decision was Sofia's higher-potential language capacity.

Within the four remaining months, Sofia needed to be staffed quickly with thirty new people. This was the last task to be completed by Budapest's center manager, who was set to leave the company toward the end of the year. In the opinion of the GBC manager, the former center manager selected people with only moderate care. To make matters more difficult, he felt the purpose of the new center was rather unclear to those responsible for staffing it. When the new center manager arrived on December 20, thirty people had been hired, but many were only part-time employees. Nevertheless, the center had been inaugurated on November 20, and InfoTech was determined to move forward despite the setback.

In the meantime, the two vice presidents had communicated the new strategy to open a satellite not only to management in Budapest but had presented the strategy in a sizable meeting open to all employees. During this meeting, they explicitly stated that lower-value tasks would be migrated to the new satellite center in Sofia and that everyone in Budapest would be redeployed to new, higher-value—and therefore more interesting and better-paid—job roles. Subsequently the new Sofia satellite employees were sent to Budapest for roughly one month to receive training and appropriate education from a dedicated training team. By March 2007, the part-time employees had either been transferred to full-time positions or were replaced. Consequently the center began operations in February 2007 after only a short delay.

**Phase 2: Reactive Migration**
From the moment the new center in Sofia opened, the different country teams from operations and the procurement contact center started gradually moving from Budapest to Sofia. Whenever an employee in Budapest voluntarily left InfoTech or switched to a higher-level job function, the old job role was terminated in Budapest and migrated to Sofia. The BBC manager described the process: "In the beginning, it wasn't really a structured transfer. The manager at that time ha[d] kind of decided that 'okay, whoever of the team leaves here . . . I'm not going to replace here but in Sofia.' So the group started to move, but with no official plan, no official ending."

The business functions relocated to Sofia were led remotely by the Budapest managers. This meant their teams were split: some were still in Budapest, and the others, all new employees, were in Sofia. Management planned to counter the anticipated difficulties of remote management by frequent site visits. However, due to company-imposed travel restrictions, InfoTech eventually decided Sofia would have to build its own management capacity locally.

In 2007 an initial test to migrate positions more rapidly was conducted. The Italy–Spain–Latin America team was shifted all at once because a new BTO account in Budapest had made it possible to redeploy all team members conjointly. InfoTech also partially reconsidered its slow-paced strategy to migrate the PCC division reactively. The head of the center (i.e., the newly appointed manager over both centers) was not satisfied with the financial performance. Consequently, the ten remaining positions in the Budapest center were immediately migrated to Sofia under the supervision of the BBC manager.

**Phase 3: Proactive Migration**
After a mild deviation from the reactive migration strategy employed during phase 2, the head of the captive center and the SPP manager formulated a new, more proactive plan in mid-2008, based on discussions with the management team and key stakeholders. Instead of continuing with the policy of slow migration through attrition, the migration strategy was accelerated. Through March 2009, all remaining lower-value positions were moved to Sofia. Accordingly, Sofia advanced from its position as a satellite center toward becoming the key center responsible for operations. Budapest moved up the InfoTech value chain and became a "center of excellence" by focusing on higher-value activities and BTO.

While the overall goal of migrating positions from one center to another was clearly communicated to all employees through multiple channels, the time line for completion was never particularly stressed. Some managers criticized this communication failure: staff change readiness might have improved by delineating a clear time line for project completion. The entire plan relied heavily on communications between leadership and employees. Management encouraged staff in Budapest to actively strive for one of the new positions available at the Sofia facility. In order to fulfill the requirements for these new, higher-end roles and activities, employees had the opportunity to educate themselves with InfoTech's support and encouragement.

InfoTech was thorough in its approach to accelerating the migration plan in phase 3. It first determined exactly which positions needed to be migrated and the current and future availability of new, higher-value job roles in Budapest. For each new role identified, managers analyzed the type of skills and experience required for the position. They also conducted a skills analysis of the remaining employees and determined which ones qualified for each position. The management team then appraised the aspirations and wishes of the employees in this regard. This assessment was then compared with both available and anticipated new job positions. On this basis, they created a best-fit scenario for all involved. The hiring process was initiated in Sofia once they came to a shift arrangement.

Two exceptional cases came about during the migration process: the transfer of PASC to Sofia and the shift of the U.K./Ireland operations team to Bangalore, India. The PASC team was not migrated to Sofia gradually, person by person, but in groups of at least five people at a time. PASC was an exception to the reactive migration strategy because the transfer of PASC job roles had not been planned at the outset of the migration operation, so no staff had been hired in Sofia to take over the tasks and individual hiring would have been inefficient.

The second anomaly was the transfer of the U.K./Ireland team. Initially the division began a gradual transfer to Sofia as planned. However, between August and September 2008, the head of the center decided to move the team to

Bangalore, which already served English-speaking markets. Cost issues were at the root of this decision. Saving money for the team was critical for the company, as the entire European center struggled to meet its financial targets. In addition to the location change, the transfer was different in that it was guided by a clearly responsible individual. As of March 2010, the center in Sofia employed just over 100 staff,and despite a few minor setbacks, the project as a whole stayed on track (figure 10.4).

## Key Challenges during the Migration of the Captive Center

Three location-specific challenge groups were identified in this study: challenges in Sofia, challenges in Budapest, and challenges in both locations, as outlined in Figure 10.5. Considering the challenges the Sofia center faced, it soon became apparent that the center's problems were all related to one topic: building a delivery capability. The challenges for the Budapest center concerned managing (logistically and psychologically) the redistribution of employees in the "old" center. Finally, the challenges that pertained to both centers can be divided into two themes: general conditions, such as center cost pressure, speed requirements, cultural differences and inexperienced teams; and collaboration issues, such as coordination and timing, remote management, and the relationship between Budapest and Sofia. As a result, four main groups of challenges were identified, providing the structure for the remainder of this chapter.

### General Conditions
High cost pressures, speed requirements, immaturity of the teams, and cultural differences were identified as the main

1. A large portion of the operations teams is migrated:

   • Italy, Spain, and Latin America are 100 percent transferred.

   • France Benelux to be complete in January 2009, except for two Dutch positions, which will shift in mid-2009.

   • Nordics are approximately 50 percent transferred and will be complete in March 2009 (except the Danish).

   • Central (Germany, Switzerland, and Austria) is 50 percent complete, scheduled to finish in March 2009.

   • U.K./Ireland is shifted to Bangalore, scheduled to be complete in January 2009.

2. PCC is 100 percent migrated (except Danish).

3. PASC just started moving and is scheduled to be complete at the end of February 2009 and combined with PCC.

   • A few business controls and one educational staff are in Sofia for support.

   • Some tasks are remaining in Budapest due to language considerations.

   • BTO accounts for approximately 25percent of all staff (70 out of 280).

   • For twelve of the twenty targeted moves, people in Budapest are redeployed to one new BTO account.

   • Fifteen new positions are available to people in Budapest.

**Figure 10.4**
Migration status as of November 2008

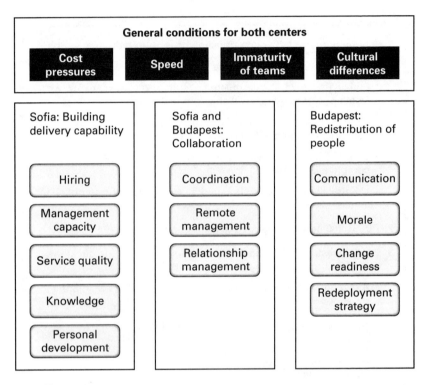

**Figure 10.5**
Migration challenges for Sofia and Budapest

challenges associated with the general preconditions of the migration and confronted both centers.

**Cost Pressures**   InfoTech is known for imposing strong cost pressure on all of its activities, and cost considerations were the main driver behind the entire migration process. Moving the PCC function from Budapest to Sofia and the last-minute move of the U.K./Ireland Operations to Bangalore clearly demonstrated the centers' strain to meet financial targets. In day-to-day business, cost pressures became especially visible in the last quarter of each year, when InfoTech typically imposed an overall expense freeze. These freezes mostly affected travel because considerable savings can be achieved relatively effortlessly in this domain. At the launch of the migration project in the last quarter of 2006, such a freeze was already in place. Ironically, management as well as newly hired staff in Sofia frequently traveled between the two centers into the beginning of 2007. In retrospect, the BBC manager admitted this constituted "inefficient" travel.

During phase 2, travel was restricted for budgetary reasons prior to the last quarter of 2008, when the extent of cost pressures was exacerbated by the global financial crisis. These travel restrictions had several effects on the overall migration project. First, personal meetings between employees of the two centers were only selectively approved, even when the employees belonged to the same team. As a consequence, collaboration often had to be conducted from a distance. Limitations in travel affected not only employees; management had to reduce its trips between the two centers as well. Moreover, the planned assignment of a manager to the Sofia facility was abandoned because of similar cost considerations, a change that created a perception of a lack of leadership in Sofia.

Finally, training efforts were problematic because of the travel restrictions. While the training team was supposed to provide Sofia with the same services as Budapest, these activities were hindered by the travel freeze. In sum, difficulties related to remoteness increased, leadership in Sofia became impaired, and training efforts were set off balance.

**Speed**   The procurement centers were required to change rather quickly. Founded in 2004, the Budapest center faced the start of this far-reaching migration after only two years of operation. Between 2006 and 2008, more than 50 percent of all employees in the Budapest center changed their job roles, and staffing in Sofia reached ninety people. "We went with full speed this year [2008] to make this happen . . . and happen fast," recalled the France Benelux business manager.

Keeping up with the rapid growth has certainly been one of the major challenges that the two InfoTech captive centers faced. Specifically, three negative consequences came about as a result of the pace set by InfoTech. First, the speed of the migration and the resulting strong growth of the Sofia center made it difficult to develop sufficient management capacity in the new center. Second, employees had to be promoted very quickly. Employees in Sofia came to expect this pace of promotion would continue, which management deemed unrealistic and caused problems later when growth flattened. Third, the BCC manager indicated that some quality problems cropped up in the Sofia center because of the pace of growth: many new employees were hired, and often they did not gain sufficient process and domain knowledge at the time the center needed it.

**Immaturity of Teams**   The employees from the Budapest and Sofia centers within all hierarchical levels were described by the interviewees as rather inexperienced. Most had been with the company only a few years, often as their first job following college. According to the Sofia center manager, the management team was also inexperienced: "Besides [the head of the center], we have nobody who has been a manager within the company for more than two to three years." This scant experience resulted in a perceived lack of leadership in

Sofia. Furthermore, the immaturity of the team amplified the problems associated with remote management. The Sofia center manager explained that the problems of remote management could be solved, "but you need very experienced people who can do it."

**Cultural Differences**   Culture management was among the most challenging factors in the migration. Apart from country culture, the InfoTech company culture created tensions during the migration. There were several reports from the people involved in the migration about how people from the two countries typically behaved.

According to the comments collected from the managers involved in the migration, Hungarians generally were seen as people who did not easily embrace change and seldom participated in a proactive, positive manner. These characteristics would have made the migration from Budapest to Sofia much more challenging. It also explains to some extent why many employees showed little enthusiasm for the new plan. The new roles offered to the Hungarian employees were more interesting and better paid than their old roles, but management had not expected people to be so comfortable with their old positions, and no one imagined they would experience difficulty inducing the Hungarians into new, more involved positions. The SPP manager stated that the underlying goal of the new career management approach was to introduce cultural change into the Budapest center. The change program was meant to drive individuals to change their behavior in order to establish a stronger link between behavior, performance, and rewards.

Management perceived the Hungarian staff as introverted people who only rarely provided proper feedback; instead they gossiped quietly. The rumors and a decline in morale and attitude that were associated with this change came as no surprise.

Bulgarians, in contrast, were commonly seen as being very direct with a positive attitude. What becomes clear in this situation is that the collaboration between the rather introverted Hungarians and the more extroverted Bulgarians caused problems. The France Benelux Team (FBT) manager stated, "Bulgarians are known to be much more direct, and Hungarians are not direct at all—more closed, introvert—and that often clashed." Specifically, cultural communication seemed to increase problems of remoteness and exacerbated existing communication difficulties. However, the GBC manager cautioned against overestimating the extent of these clashes: "I cannot say that there were huge disasters. . . . It's sometimes interesting, sometimes annoying, let's be honest . . . but it is simply something we have to [deal with]."

Apart from country culture, the issue of corporate culture and its effect on change at InfoTech was discussed during the management interviews. In contrast to country culture, people judged InfoTech's business culture as strongly favoring change. This was exemplified by the FBT manager: "I think a lot of people realize that whenever you want to make a change, you can do that at InfoTech. . . . There is always a possibility. That was my main drive to continue with this company."

This atmosphere had historic roots. InfoTech had undergone an extreme change from a hardware company twenty years ago to a company that provides a range of services and products. As a result of multiple organizational and structural changes, employees at InfoTech, especially those at the center in Budapest, became accustomed to change rather quickly. The Nordic team manager shared her thoughts on the subject, stating, "It could be a kind of 'branding' to the center that we are adapting to change quickly and quite well."

The importance ascribed to change management was highlighted when the consulting part of the company was acquired some years ago. "When we bought [the captive unit]," stated the head of the center, "we got a lot of consultants, and among others, a lot of change consultants, [which] has affected the culture in InfoTech. I mean, the methodologies introduced by these people were . . . widespread."

This positive attitude toward change is also reflected in InfoTech's policies toward underperforming employees. Rather than terminating underperformers, considerable effort is put into staff development. "If we have a bad performer," stated the BBC manager, "we need to change that. Firing somebody is not a solution. We need to change the person. And only if we are unable to change that person, then we have to start that [termination] process." InfoTech is said to be a very social employer in general: "InfoTech has a culture where it is really humane to the people. So, only once in a blue moon, we fire people. We don't fire people. We don't know how to fire people, basically."

This policy represented a major reason behind why the migration was initially conducted gradually and why every person whose position was migrated to Sofia was redeployed instead of terminated. However, the message to be a humane and change-favoring company has not necessarily embedded itself in the mind-set of the Budapest or Sofia staff yet. The FBT manager expresses the issue succinctly: "It takes time for people to grasp . . . that you can change things. So, I think the level of maturity is not there yet." Although this message has not yet fully integrated itself into the culture of the two centers, InfoTech is a benevolent company that favors change and progress and has a benevolent attitude toward its employees.

### Challenges for Sofia: Building a Delivery Capacity

Against the backdrop of these general conditions, the migration project caused several other challenges in Sofia. Among the most critical factors that affected delivery capability, we identified hiring, management capacity, personal development and career path, knowledge, and service quality.

**Hiring**   From the outset, it was clear that finding employees in Sofia who could support countries with less common language sets would be difficult due to Sofia's smaller targeted labor pool. German and French speakers could be hired easily within approximately six weeks and a whole team within around three months, but Danish, Dutch, and Finnish speakers were considerably harder to find. The Sofia site manager estimated a time span of around three to four months as a more realistic expectation, but without any guarantee for success. This issue was so pressing that one interviewee even noted that the center began hiring for language capabilities rather than for other targeted skills.

Not only were the rarer languages hard to find in Sofia, but there was also stiff competition in the job market. The Sofia site manager called the market in Bulgaria "extremely dynamic. . . . A person interviewed this week might already have another job next week." This significant time pressure made coordination with Budapest to move people into new roles very challenging.

One final reason for the difficulties in hiring was Sofia's diminished attractiveness in comparison to Budapest. External recruits were much more difficult to obtain because of this factor. In fact, only two internal members relocated from Budapest to Sofia, mainly for a job promotion. In order to find a possible solution to the challenge, InfoTech proposed conducting a search using outside agencies. Using this method, the top teams in Sofia and Budapest were confident they would be able to meet the staffing deadline, when all remaining low-value tasks were to be moved to Sofia.

In sum, an extremely dynamic and competitive labor market, hard-to-find language skills, and the less attractive location in Sofia caused difficulties in hiring new staff. These factors led to timing and coordination problems and slowed the migration process.

**Management Capacity**   Overall, the management of both centers was rather inexperienced. Apart from the head of the center, no other team member had been a manager within the company for more than two to three years, and all employees from Budapest had joined not more than five years ago.

Although the management team in Budapest worked smoothly, there was a perceived lack of leadership at the Sofia center. One explanation for this perception was the fact that only two managers were appointed to Sofia to oversee almost one hundred employees. In addition, management in Budapest was still responsible for the newly hired staff in Sofia and had to accomplish their task remotely. Sofia management was not developed from the outset because, according to the FBT manager, such strong, rapid growth had not been anticipated: "It was more of a pilot. They . . . never consider[ed] moving PCC and PASC" in the beginning. In retrospect, however, adequate management needs should have been addressed for the Sofia site from the very beginning.

Growth in Sofia had come about too fast to keep up with developing talents. According to the Sofia site manager, not enough capacity was available: "You don't make a manager overnight. That doesn't happen from today to tomorrow. It takes some time." Furthermore, the jobs in the Sofia center were the very first ones for many of the newly recruited employees. However, the Sofia site manager maintained that within about six months, some very talented young people should be ready to take on managerial roles.

An additional reason for the scarce management resources in Sofia was an obligation, imposed by InfoTech culture, to hire internally. According to the SPP manager, "The plan at that time was not hiring externally . . . but [to use] internal team leaders and managers because . . . we will need people who know the operation inside and out [who] don't have to learn InfoTech from the beginning." Because the center was new, InfoTech culture had to be introduced. Moreover the two centers needed to work together very closely, so building management internally was a strategic priority.

**Personal Development and Career Path**   In accordance with the fast growth of the two centers and the decision to appoint management from the inside, promotional opportunities came about extremely quickly for many employees. "Obviously, when you grow next year to double the size, you need double the amount of team leads . . . and they were chosen from the group of people that we had started with initially," the FBT manager explained. This created enormous promotion expectations that realistically could not be sustained into the future, as the center would eventually reach a natural saturation point. Managing employee expectations became crucial in an attempt to avoid high attrition.

This issue, however, has been managed well thus far; in 2008, there was still relatively low turnover.

**Knowledge** Knowledge-related issues were one of the critical challenges in this migration. The first of these problems related to the issue of knowledge transfer from Budapest to Sofia. "When we move people here in Budapest to new job roles, we need Sofia to be ready to take over the 'old' task. Here, a big challenge is how to do the knowledge transfer," the head of the center stated. The GBC manager agreed, but stressed that a certain loss of experience was natural in such a transition.

The training of new employees in Sofia was a general concern. The training team in Budapest initially planned to provide Sofia staff with the same services as they had for the Budapest center. For newcomers, this would involve human resources introduction training, general process training, general procurement process training, Enterprise Resource Planning (ERP) training, and operations-specific SAP training. After the introductory training had been accomplished, on-the-job training usually involved advanced procurement skills training and soft skill courses (e.g., project management or customer treatment). During the first phase, new employees were supposed to travel to Budapest for introduction training. Later, the training team would visit Sofia to support employee education on location. However, these activities were derailed by the travel freeze, as trips for the trainers and new employees were extremely limited. According to the education team leader, training could not be conducted in the best way.

Two further challenges related to knowledge management and training: pace and scheduling. First, it appeared the pace of the training was intense. "One thing the people here [in Budapest] tend to forget, especially those . . . who have been here for a longer time, [is] that we had a much longer training. . . . Now we try to train the buyers in one or two weeks," explained the GBC manager. Second, scheduling training for the people who moved to higher-value job roles was difficult due to the split demand: "It's becoming so fractured," said the SPP manager. "There is not a critical mass of people that are going in one place where I can start giving them training." Of the two demands, the latter was more of a challenge at the Budapest center, where people who switched to higher-value job roles needed specific training.

This challenge with education was resolved to a large extent by placing one education team member at the Sofia center on a regular basis. This meant a promotion, and thus the relocation was voluntary.

**Service Quality**    Finally, one of the most critical tasks in the migration was to conduct the entire change without affecting the quality of service provided to customers. Because the service in Sofia was supposed to be exactly the same as in Budapest, customers should not have noticed any difference. Nevertheless, customers recognized that the service location had moved. This realization came about in part because customers had built up personal relationships with the former job owners in Budapest. According to the Sofia site manager, customers complained at the beginning of the migration, even if the service quality was the same, most likely because of the loss of the personal connection they had established with staff in Budapest. InfoTech considered reestablishing these relationships as one of the top priorities for the Sofia staff.

The FBT manager also recognized the potential service quality issue when the migration was announced. New to the center at that time, he noticed people were more concerned about service quality than about their own jobs, an attitude toward quality that impressed him. This unexpected response stemmed from the fact that the center faced many complaints from internal clients at that time. Employees were used to working with colleagues in the same building, not collaborating remotely. It was difficult for the staff to see how the additional complexity of a split center could be overcome. In reaction to quality concerns, the business controls department increased control over the Sofia center. Instead of the usual quality control sample size of process orders (5 percent), a higher sample size was established for Sofia in order to ensure proper quality monitoring. According to the GBC manager, Sofia performed relatively well, especially at the outset. Consequently, testing in Sofia was later reduced to normal levels. Today control samples are randomly selected between Hungary and Sofia.

Unfortunately, at the beginning of 2008, "the number of defects in the process increased," according to the GBC manager. The reason was thought to be the rapid growth of the center and the number of inexperienced new employees. In order to control and monitor the situation, two people from the business controls department were placed in Sofia on one-year assignments.

The situation for PCC was somewhat different; there was a point in time when the targets were clearly not met. "Most of the things were 'red': we had a lot of abandoned calls; clients were complaining. Then, [the head of the center] came and said, `This has to be fixed,'" acknowledged the BBC manager. This resulted in the decision to move the function quickly and completely to Sofia instead of continuing with the gradual process. According to the BBC manager, everything "turned green" after only a few months following completion of the move.

Apart from PCC, the transition did not affect the quality of the work in a negative way. On an aggregated level, the GBC manager agreed, stating, "I don't think the Bulgarian team is worse or better than the Hungarian team. It's really the same, actually. What's lost . . . during the operational team transition is a bit of experience. But this is something normal."

### Challenges for Budapest: Managing the Redistribution of People

While Sofia faced problems setting up the necessary capabilities and capacities to deliver service successfully, the Budapest center was mainly challenged with redistributing employees from lower-value to higher-level job roles. From a psychological point of view, it was difficult to keep up the overall morale in the center and encourage people to become adaptive to change. Appropriate communication was a key factor to success in this regard. Redeployment also represented an organizational challenge the company needed to overcome.

**Communication** Communication was one of the most serious challenges the teams faced during all three phases of migration. At the beginning of the transition in phase 1, the top-down communication was not entirely convincing. Although at an all-hands meeting, executives clearly stated that only lower-value tasks would go to Sofia and everyone in Budapest would be redeployed, many people did not believe them. Instead, rumors flourished, and the morale in the center dropped. Local management appeared rather passive in its communication during that time. Moreover, employees were barely involved in the process as a whole. In this respect, one manager stated, "There were bits of communication, a lot of rumors, and I guess people made a lot of assumptions. So, a lot of what actually happened was discussed in meeting rooms, with the management, [and] some of it trickled down to the teams, but the message was not really out there."

During phase 2, communication efforts by management were moderate by comparison. As people in Budapest noticed that new job roles were indeed coming to the center, anxiety diminished. However, at the same time, the first problems with remote management arose. This represented one main reason that the pace of migration picked up and communication was increased during phase 3.

Increased communication was one of the most striking differences of the new approach implemented during phase 3. During the career management campaign, InfoTech emphasized the message that people should start taking responsibility for their careers and autonomously look for new roles and educate themselves accordingly. In other words, those who had made the transition into different job roles had to become proactive, and people in general needed to prepare for future shifts—a significant cultural change.

In order to get the message across, four information sessions were conducted in Budapest and two in Sofia. Apart from open meetings, this also involved a "mini career week," where colleagues who were already placed in the new, higher-value jobs presented their work. Furthermore, various avenues of communication were opened up: intensified newsletter work; setting up intranet information, presentations, and posters; and arranging personal meetings between staff and managers.

Although the new approach was viewed as a success, concerns remained. That people remained somewhat skeptical about the center's ability to move up the value chain was reflected in the rather low participation rate in the information sessions.[4] While many thought that there was not enough communication during phases 1 and 2, some people complained about too much communication during phase 3.

Despite recent successes, the head of the center still perceived that the biggest challenge was to get people more excited about the project as a whole. The SPP manager worked on a marketing plan to stimulate interest about career development and create a more positive atmosphere.

**Employee Morale**   Going through times of intense change in most cases imposes stress on an organization and often leads to a decline in employee morale. The psychological state of the people in Budapest was a major challenge during this transition.

In phase 1, even prior to the official news release regarding the new center in Sofia, numerous rumors were floating around the Budapest center. When the actual strategy was finally announced in a meeting to all employees, it was stated clearly that everyone would be redeployed within the center. Despite this unambiguous announcement, morale immediately plummeted: employees did not believe management and feared losing their jobs.

In phase 2, when new employees from Sofia arrived at the Budapest center for training, the Hungarian personnel finally began to accept the new situation. They realized that the promised jobs would indeed come to their center. This was especially true when sourcing hub positions were introduced in addition to the less esteemed BTO roles.[5] People were relieved. Nevertheless, there were still problems with the redeployment in Budapest and job matching with the hiring in Sofia, and a certain level of fear remained with respect to job loss.

In phase 3, with the initiation of the new plan to move all remaining tasks to Sofia and redeploy people in Budapest to new roles, the atmosphere finally changed. Although people remained somewhat skeptical about the transition, the general mood was on the rise. Furthermore, the increased level of communication helped improve the atmosphere. One manager observed, "Last year was a lot of just looking at our pain points, a lot of just making things work. And now that we have a team in place, we can really focus on creating value."

**Change Readiness** Tightly connected to the mood of the teams was their general lack of readiness for the announced change, although some people had become accustomed to change. On a general level, employees in Budapest were willing to take on new roles even though their cultural background was not in favor of such a change for three main reasons. First and foremost, the pace of transformation had been so high during the previous years that they simply had to adapt. Second, the employees in Budapest were, on average, much younger than employees in the InfoTech country organizations and therefore were inherently more flexible. Finally, interviewees stated that many employees perceived the lower-value job roles as boring. According to the BBC manager, "These administrative profiles are now very monotone for our people." The FBT manager agreed: "No one wants to stay in the low-value positions longer than two or three years. People want to move on to new job roles."

Nevertheless people in Budapest remained somewhat skeptical about changing positions. This skepticism mainly concerned the new plan to move the skills in Budapest up the value chain and establish it as a center of excellence. Although people were becoming more open to change, they were not entirely convinced about the new strategy. The head of the center stated, "As an organization, we are continuously moving. So, in that sense, I think the center is very change-ready. In the other sense, to be ready also to move up the value chain and not just to change, I think it has been a little bit more difficult. . . . I think the mentality here is a little bit reluctant. . . . The most difficult thing for me is to get people excited about moving up the value chain."

To overcome this skepticism, management finally motivated employees to be open to change by promoting career opportunities and financial benefits. Moving to a higher-value job role coincided with more interesting job assignments and moving up in the company hierarchy. Although the two benefits were attractive to employees, they were more interested in career opportunities than in higher salaries. For example, one manager perceived career development as the main motivation for employees to change: "It is not about money. Well, okay, don't underestimate the financial aspect of the situation, but it is not *always* about money. If you have a job opportunity for career development within your country, you will achieve the financial step of your desires anyways." The FBT manager, in contrast, judged the financial benefits to be the main driver for young employees at the beginning of their careers.

While employees in Budapest were principally ready for change, they were still skeptical about the new plan to move the skills base in the center up the value chain. In order to motivate them, InfoTech offered a mix of financial incentives and career development opportunities.

**Redeployment**  The redeployment of employees lay at the core of InfoTech's migration strategy, especially in phase 3. This process was challenging because the new job roles— especially BTO and sourcing hub—were not coming to Budapest as fast as originally anticipated. Consequently, there was not an open position for every person whose job was slated for migration, and the result was a drop in morale. In addition, it was difficult to staff positions that were available; not only were employees less motivated than expected, but training was hampered by the expense freeze.

Another aspect of redeployment was the extent to which people shifted positions voluntarily. The Sofia site manager stated; "Well, we try to redeploy those people. They have some options, some opportunities. If they are not okay, we try to redeploy them in another position, or you try to offer them another option, another opportunity. But on the other hand, if they are not—let's say if they don't accept the opportunities and don't want to look for other opportunities at the company—you can't do too much."

While InfoTech implemented numerous career, informational, and educational programs in order to motivate staff to train for and accept the higher-level jobs that were coming into the center, redeployment remained a serious challenge throughout the migration process.

### Challenges for Both Centers: Collaboration

The main challenges both centers faced as they learned to work together were centered around remote management, coordination and timing, organizational and reporting structure, and the relationships between people from Budapest and Sofia.

**Remote Management**  During the course of the migration, most of the teams became split: one portion was staffed in

Budapest and the other in Sofia. Some managers, as a consequence, had people on their teams they had never even met. InfoTech, which has a collaborative culture, heavily invested in remote collaboration capabilities such as telephone conferencing, instant messaging, and e-mail systems. Nevertheless, the felt distance between the two centers continued to cause concerns. The issue was heavily intertwined with other challenges that the two centers faced.

The key challenges relating to remote management were:

- Communication difficulties
- Cultural differences and culture clashes
- Unclear responsibility
- A lack of control
- Inexperienced management teams
- Travel restrictions
- Unclear planning and organization
- Lack of face-to-face contact

With the exception of the issue of responsibility, which is discussed below, all of these factors have previously been described. It therefore becomes clear that a sense of distance was a central problem that lay at the very heart of the migration issues.

### Coordination and Timing

The combination of coordinating and timing the hiring in Sofia with the job transitions in Budapest was the biggest challenge in the migration process. While Budapest waited to transfer employees to new, higher-value job roles, the facility in Sofia never knew in advance how many applicants they would get for the migrated position, how many would be interviewed, or how many of those screened candidates would even be suitable. This problem was compounded in the case of the even more unpredictable positions that required advanced language skills.

Budapest had just as much difficulty with internal job transitioning. Particularly at the beginning, there were not enough new positions to accommodate everyone right away. One underlying cause for this was that BTO roles were coming in more slowly than expected. When BTO finally took off and employees were needed, Sofia could not hire and train fast enough. This issue resulted in service problems and sullied the mood of the employees in both centers.

In order to address the problem, InfoTech developed and applied a more flexible approach. Although clear deadlines for individual transitions had been set, managers had to remain flexible in staffing certain positions. If a perfect match could not be found within the expected time frame, people were kept occupied in other ways, such as training or project work.

### Organizational and Reporting Structure

Remote management was one reason for problems with responsibility. According to the Nordic team manager, it was not always clear to whom to report or where to get approval because of the split between Budapest and Sofia.

On a more general level, InfoTech's structure itself seemed to entail a certain potential for confusion. The company was principally structured in a matrix system. A traditional matrix can inherently lead to unclear responsibilities in its own right, and the situation was even more complex for some of the new roles coming to Budapest. The SPP manager explained that the sourcing hub, for example, reported to three different layers. She critically acknowledged that such complex structures require clearer responsibilities.

Even when examining the microlevel of an individual migration, responsibilities were not entirely clear. According to the Sofia site manager, there was always one responsible person for each employee's shift, and the FBT manager perceived the process as a flexible agreement between the two managers directly involved. However, the question of responsibility became much clearer in later phases of the transition. In phase 3, the head of the center and the SPP manager were identified by many respondents as key drivers of the transition. Furthermore, there was an apparently clear change agent for both the India transfer and with the PCC migration.

### Relationship Management between Budapest and Sofia

The final challenge is the relationship that existed between Budapest and Sofia. Employees in Budapest charged that the expected new job roles were not migrating to them because the newly hired employees in Sofia were "stealing our jobs." Bulgarians, in contrast, felt they were being treated as second-class employees and separate from the prioritized center in Budapest. The resulting conflicts were aggravated by cultural differences and the distance between the teams.

Today the relationships between the centers have stabilized. The education team leader noted, "I can see that there still are some problems, but that's rather individual."

### Conclusion

In the course of this chapter, the main challenges relating to the migration of service center functions from Budapest to Sofia were described in detail. Many of these issues were

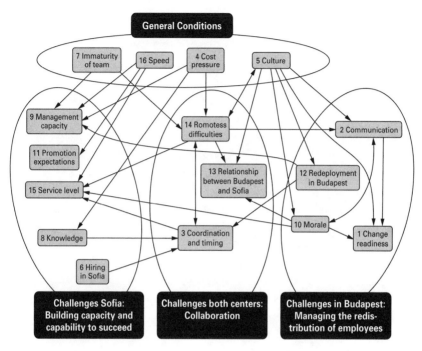

**Figure 10.6**
Challenges of the InfoTech migration

tightly interconnected. The connections between and among the issues discussed are set out in figure 10.6. Issues are linked by arrows to indicate a causal influence.

These interdependencies are complex and potentially overwhelming for two young captive centers. Yet InfoTech managed to remediate these challenges and avoid a potentially disastrous result, primarily by remaining flexible and tackling problems as they arose. InfoTech managers and executives were able to recognize these problems and adjust their strategies to provide timely and successful solutions to the complex issues that migrating captives faced.

# 11 The Way Forward: Captive Center Capabilities and Strategies

Throughout the previous chapters, we have explored the reasons for offshoring, the vehicles for offshoring, and many of the challenges that firms encounter when they choose to move business activities to captive centers. The companies examined in this book provide a foundation for making some generalizations about captive center capabilities and strategies moving forward into the future. This chapter explores those capabilities and strategies in-depth using the research we conducted as evidence to support our conclusions.

## Setting Up a Basic Captive Center

We begin with the basic captive center, which provides services to the parent firm. This center typically covers a line of business functions such as back office services, software development and maintenance, and call centers. In many of the cases we studied, the decision to offshore through a captive center was motivated primarily by cost-cutting opportunities. Up to 30 percent of business costs can be saved through the offshoring of business processes.[1] Our study of GlobalAirline confirms this observation.

Nevertheless, there are challenges along the offshoring journey that will cause these potential savings to evaporate if they are not well addressed. One key challenge is the ability of the captive center to attract and retain talent in a dynamic market for skills and expertise.

Although an offshore vendor enjoys a 15 percent arbitrage in setting up costs in comparison to those incurred by the offshore captive center, the captive center option still has the advantage of being in control of internal business processes. For example, an information technology (IT) capability may be poorly serviced in the offshore market by a local vendor, whereas the parent firm possesses deep domain knowledge and advanced resources to set up and manage an offshore captive center. As one expert stated, "[The process] was and is the blood of the organization. Therefore, keeping control of this process was an essential criterion."

To sum up, the decision to establish a basic captive center is driven by the desire to maintain control over a particular process, perceived cost savings, the lack of highly developed services offered by an offshore service provider, and the perception that the parent firm has the resources and capabilities to set up and manage the offshore center (figure 11.1).[2]

All the basic captive centers we studied have evolved into a new form, rewriting their objectives. Some have added

**Figure 11.1**
Key drivers for setting up a captive center

higher-value services to their service portfolio and moved up the value chain, while others have offloaded some of their offshore assets or services to refocus their strategic position in the offshore market. Both parent firms and captive centers were involved in reshaping the role that the captive center played in the firm's global strategy and operational approach.

Some firms consider additional operational concepts in their captive centers. ITConsulting's captive center was set up not only to perform back office work but also to centralize processes. Clearly such settings address management's agenda to introduce change in the organization by moving certain business processes into an offshore location and centralizing services across several geographic and product units. The captive center in this case evolved as a center of excellence for a particular line of services.

When these three categories of factors—exogenous factors, catalyst factors, and the business environment—are brought together, the framework in table 11.1 can be offered.[3]

With these frameworks in mind, we now explore the key challenges associated with setting up a basic captive center.

### The Key Challenges in Setting Up a Captive Center

Basic captive centers face two distinct challenges: the relationship with the parent firm and the ability of the center to build up scale.

The first challenge, developing relationships with the parent firm, encompasses several aspects. First, relationships with the parent firm concern the business model and therefore the mentality that the captive center pursues. Quite often captive centers are treated as cost centers. This

**Table 11.1**
Factors influencing the decision to set up a captive center

| Exogenous factors | Catalyst factors | Business environment |
| --- | --- | --- |
| Availability of sophisticated outsourcers | Time zone replacement (24/7 work) | Keeping control |
| Government regulations and tax breaks | Cultural understanding (e.g., GlobalAirline) | Process coordination |
| Infrastructure (communication) | Labor pool | Cost advantages |
| Educational system | Language proficiency | Sending back office work to free up captive center staff Creating service mind-set |

*Source:* Vashistha and Vashistha (2006).

approach originates from the initial and sometimes ongoing investments required by the parent firm to ensure that back office services provided by the captive center are on par with onshore standards. The relationship with the parent firm is often based on efficiencies in performance, which demonstrates the limited interest that the parent firm often has regarding the potential development of the captive center beyond its basic form. GlobalAirline is a good example of this mentality, though this captive center and its evolutionary path (i.e., how it developed over time) can be considered a success.[4] Clearly, in the case of GlobalAirline, both the acquiring firm and the captive center changed this mentality and began considering the captive center as a profit center.

The challenge of attracting commitment to the development of the captive center is critical in this respect. This

challenge is well illustrated in the ITConsulting and ConsumerGoods cases. At the same time, the GlobalAirline case
demonstrates that a lack of commitment can actually help a
captive center choose its own management structure and
run its operations independent from the parent company.

The second challenge concerns captive centers' ability to
build scale. Several factors can have a negative effect on this
ability, starting with the parent firm's belief that the offshored process is core to its competitiveness, which serves
to limit the captive center's ability to serve external clients.[5]
As one expert explained, "They [the captive centers] also
have a problem of being subscaled if they haven't defined
the scale upfront." The former general manager of the GlobalAirline captive center concurred: "I think the main disadvantage was they could not see their way to get to critical
scale." The other reason for this scale deficiency is the parent
firm's unwillingness to invest in the captive center beyond
the minimum required to maintain the same level of service
as was provided from onshore. An example of this attitude
is seen in the case of GlobalAirline, as one executive
exclaimed: "We are running an airline; we are not in an
investment house."

Clearly basic captive centers also face typical outsourcing
challenges, such as cultural problems, cooperation issues,
language problems, security issues, high staff turnover, attrition rates, and wage increases, as in any offshore outsourcing
engagement. In our studies, we have seen how these challenges can have a critical impact on the captive center's
ability to deliver high-quality service. For example, Global-
Software faced difficulties offering 24/7 work when staff
became demotivated, which led to rising attrition rates.
The process improvement and performance management
director for GlobalSoftware recognized that "if we have a lot

of attrition, we do not get domain knowledge," which could hamper the captive center's desire to develop and attract external clients. Others, such as one expert we interviewed, pointed out that it can be much more challenging to attract needed talent than to retain an adequate talent level simply because of the high turnover rates businesses have experienced in offshore locations such as India. Furthermore, labor turnover often increases as new employees at a captive center find that their work tasks are boring and repetitive and offer no challenges.

Besides the high turnover rates, wage increases in labor markets are also a problem, as in the case of Consumer-Goods. Clearly there are still opportunities mainly deriving from cost differences in many offshore locations; however, these are eroding because of wage inflation. We believe that India will maintain its attractiveness as an offshoring destination into the near future.[6]

Achieving smooth communication between distant locations can be a major challenge for captive centers.[7] Some companies, such as AmeriBank and ITConsulting, addressed this problem by not sending specific tasks that needed close communications to their offshore captive center or by ensuring that the staff offshore had the necessary skills. However, all of the firms we studied faced communication challenges that derived from either use of different languages or cultural differences.

Finally, the cultural fit of the captive center and the parent firm needs to be addressed in some manner. GlobalAirline and ConsumerGoods avoided cultural clashes because both already had operations in India when they set up their captive centers. None of the other firms we studied had dramatic cultural problems. One reason could be that these were global companies used to dealing with cultural differences.

## How to Cope with the Challenges

To overcome the key challenges that a basic captive center may face, such as scale and the relationship with the parent firm, the center should be set up as a commercial organization and structured as a profit center. It should have a mission statement, clear objectives, and a business plan, which needs to be revisited from time to time. The plan should not necessarily seek growth; more important, it should be designed to ensure sustainability and profitability. Bringing all stakeholders together during the decision-making process with respect to setting up the captive center is critical, as well as when revisiting the objects and targets of the captive center.

A higher degree of integration between the captive center and the parent firm will allow the center to explore growth opportunities. Captive centers should not be established merely to deal with the basic back office work. As centers ramp up their skills base, they become capable of performing higher-value activities.

When it comes to more commonly found challenges associated with offshoring, such as high attrition rates, the responsibility lies with the captive center's top team to carefully screen and select staff and offer a career path, bonus systems, and other incentives for employees. However, it will be challenging for the captive center to retain talent over time unless the center considers its evolutionary path and strategic options. For example, under certain conditions, the center could shift its focus to developing new services (e.g., through insourcing), while outsourcing offshored services from the captive center to local vendors.

## Capabilities a Basic Captive Center Should Develop

We believe there are two sets of capabilities for captive centers to develop: necessary capabilities and additional capabilities (table 11.2).

**Table 11.2**
Capabilities for basic captive centers

| Necessary capabilities | Additional capabilities |
|---|---|
| Organizational design | Sourcing |
| Internal customer development | Sales and marketing |
| Planning and internal contracting | Business development |
| Governance | |
| Domain expertise | |

Necessary capabilities are those that concern the relationship between the captive center and the parent firm. Setting up proper governance structures to deliver services to the parent and developing domain expertise in the specific area of the business process will serve the captive center only in its evolutionary path. Having developed these capabilities, the captive center will be perceived by the parent firm as a center of excellence that can branch out beyond the firm's clientele base. However, some capabilities, such as sourcing and business development and sales and marketing, are not core to the daily operations of the basic captive center. These will become necessary capabilities once the captive center embarks on its own evolutionary path.

---

*Captive center–specific motives*   Availability of sophisticated outsourcers and reliable infrastructure offshore is limited; supportive government regulations and tax breaks; need for control over specific processes; low complexity of coordination
*Offshoring motives*   Financial benefits; labor pool; availability of skills

---

*Advantages of large companies* Strong brand names that attract talented labor
*Basic captive center–specific challenges* Building scale; shaping relationships with the parent firm
*Generic offshoring challenges* Attrition levels; language and culture issues; security problems; wage increases
*Basic captive center–specific solutions* Standardize processes ; define governance model and roles; set up the captive as a commercially driven unit; move up the value chain; define and communicate clear goals and roles; revisit business plan
*Developed capabilities* Organizational design; governance; business management; domain expertise; leadership

## Evolving into a Hybrid Captive Center

The hybrid captive center is based on the concept that offshored activities performed by the captive center will be carried out by a local vendor as either an outsourcing or an insourcing arrangement. Short-term assignments can be outsourced or insourced, while long-term assignments are more likely to be outsourced. The main strategic implication for long-term outsourcing assignments is the captive center's ability to develop sophisticated sourcing capabilities offshore.

A basic captive center that evolves into a hybrid captive center and seeks to outsource some specific activities for a short term is unlikely to develop strong sourcing capabilities offshore. Therefore, insourcing may emerge as a better option to ensure that the local vendor and the client are working together within the same physical space and avoiding challenges that crop up with distance. When a basic captive center is considering sourcing out an entire business process, such as hosting services, the nature, magnitude, and implications for the parent firm require the captive center to develop sophisticated sourcing capabilities offshore. The outsourcing option therefore becomes more attractive as the captive center successfully manages its vendor, regardless of the physical distance.

The hybrid captive option allows the captive center to free up talent to move to higher-value activities and therefore reposition its contribution within the firm's global strategy. Some companies that pursued the hybrid captive center option have developed new products following this change, and some continued along this evolutionary path and pursued a market-driven approach by attracting external clients. The option to develop a basic captive center into a hybrid captive center should be based on the factors outlined in figure 11.2, which considers the outsourcing capabilities available in the captive center, the maturity of the local vendor market in terms of the line of services that the captive center provides and the opportunity for the center to shift its focus to deliver high-value services and products.

The sourcing of offshored business functions brings additional benefits to the captive center. For example, GlobalSoftware's captive center benefited from its outsourcing arrangement with the vendor in two ways. First, the center paid for only the services actually delivered by the service provider. Second, it benefited from methodologies applied and innovations introduced by the outsourcing firm as the relationships between the two tightened over time. Furthermore, the switch to a hybrid captive center model allowed the captive center's top management to gain exposure to the local vendor market, which had served the captive center

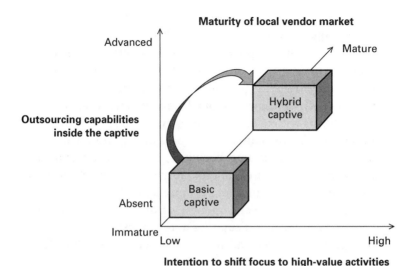

**Figure 11.2**
Why outsource offshored activities? Shift to high-value activities, maturity, and outsourcing capabilities

well as its top team was considering how it might develop over time. Such partnerships in the early stages of the captive center's development are critical to its ability to evolve into a shared captive center or for considering a divestment option.

### The Key Challenges for Hybrid Captive Center: Learn How to Source

Developing sourcing capabilities offshore and ensuring the same (or better) level of service from the vendor are the key challenges for hybrid captive centers. Clearly these two challenges are linked because the ability to ensure same-level service from a local vendor requires advanced sourcing capabilities in the offshore location. A basic captive center is not likely to possess these capabilities, and developing them can be rather lengthy and difficult. This can be even more complex for hybrid captive centers, which often outsource to a local vendor that is located nearby, which may result in a loose approach to governance and contracting. This is particularly true in the case of GlobalSoftware, where existing problems with the outsourced services were exacerbated following implementation of the outsourcing contract. The vendor inherited existing problems; however, it assumed that because of the physical proximity, solving the problems during transition would not be a problem. This was proven wrong; only after several months of dissatisfaction on all sides did the client and supplier agree to restart the change management process and address the knowledge transfer process.

The concern about service levels may spill over from the captive center to the parent firm. In such situations, the parent firm might feel it is losing control over processes that it considers central to its success.

The more the hybrid captive center outsources or insources activities, the more it will need to become a sophisticated outsourcing player. This will also raise a concern by the parent firm regarding duplication of this capability, as most firms develop strong sourcing capabilities onshore. However, since a good relationship between clients and vendors is one of the key factors that drives success in outsourcing arrangements, sourcing capabilities need to be developed offshore to meet unique circumstances and arrangements. For example, GlobalSoftware encountered difficulties when outsourcing nonstandardized tasks to its Indian vendor. It had to develop solutions offshore in the form of contract management and relationship management to ensure that the vendor team could work closely with the client to retain knowledge and deliver service. As these sourcing management solutions emerged offshore at the captive center, the contribution of the parent firm was limited. The lesson is that captive centers should develop strong sourcing capabilities offshore despite any duplication with such capabilities onshore. At the same time, captive centers should refrain from assuming that because their vendor is local, they do not need strong sourcing management capabilities.

Finally, as the hybrid captive center frees up talent for higher-value activities, it needs the parent firm's support and commitment to offer its staff challenging projects. Our research shows that parent firms do not always offer this commitment. Most still view the captive center as a cost center and fail to see its potential for generating innovations, new products, and new services.

### Hybrid Captive Center: How to Cope with These Challenges

Because the main challenge for the hybrid captive center is to develop sourcing capabilities and ensure the same or better service levels, our advice is simple: learn, and learn fast. The starting point should be to prepare a business case to the parent firm in which the revised business plan of the captive center is presented and in which the expected outcomes from this change process are outlined against existing performance.

The captive center will need to develop a pilot program that will allow it to experiment with outsourcing prior to launching a relatively large outsourcing contract. Pilot projects should allow the center to harvest best practices as well as identify arrangements and structures that do not work well. A dedicated team should monitor the learning gained and document the results from each pilot project.

We recommend that captive centers considering their first relatively large outsourcing contract use the services of an intermediary firm to ensure that all aspects have been carefully examined. As the captive center becomes more proficient in executing outsourcing contracts and as their staff shift focus to work on new ideas, we recommend the center redesign its organizational structure and separate the service and sourcing arm from the innovative arm of the unit.

**What Capabilities a Hybrid Captive Center Should Develop**

First and foremost, hybrid captive centers should develop the same necessary capabilities as a basic captive . In addition, it needs sourcing management capabilities to manage its sourcing arrangements.

Hybrid captive centers also need to develop innovation management capabilities that will allow their staff to shift focus from a service mentality to the development of new opportunities in the form of new services and products. As they focus on new opportunities, they should seek partnerships and alliances with local vendors to speed up the process of learning about markets and competition. We suggest that the center also develop business development capabilities.

Hybrid captive centers can also develop capabilities that will prepare them as a preparation for the next step in its evolutionary path. For example, they can evolve into a shared captive center, specializing in a particular service. In this case, the captive center will need to develop marketing and sales capabilities to attract external clients. These are outlined in table 11.3.

**Table 11.3**
Capabilities for hybrid captive centers

| Necessary capabilities | Additional capabilities |
| --- | --- |
| Basic captive center capabilities | Marketing and sales |
| Sourcing management | |
| Innovation management | |
| Business development | |

*Hybrid captive center strategies*   Insourcing or outsourcing
*Hybrid captive center challenges*   Developing sourcing capabilities offshore; ensuring the same (or a better) level of service; getting support from the parent firm for future development
*Coping strategies*   Set up several outsourcing projects as pilots to learn quickly; use intermediaries for the first projects; recruit sourcing specialists; separate the innovation arm from the service-oriented arm
*Developed capabilities*   Sourcing management; innovation management; business development

## Evolving into a Shared Captive Center

Captive centers can evolve into shared captive centers from either the basic or the hybrid model. The shared captive center by definition shares services with both external and internal clients. As such, there are two drivers to becoming a shared captive center: becoming a specialist unit in a particular line of services and moving up the value chain, and increasing scale (see figure 11.3). Becoming a specialist BPO unit such as Genpact will attract additional clients and also benefit the parent firm as the captive center learns from

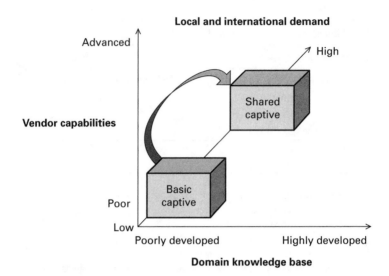

**Figure 11.3**
Why evolve into a shared captive center? Demand, specialization, and
vendor capabilities

multiple engagements and offers advanced services to both
its parent firm and external clients.

By increasing scale, the shared captive center will become
competitive as the cost of a unit processed offshore decreases.
A large scale of transactions will also position the shared
captive center as a potential target for acquisition by a local
vendor.

In our research, the GlobalAirline and ITConsulting
captive centers decided to offer services to external clients,
mainly because they sought to increase the scale of transactions processed offshore and considered penetrating new
markets by making their services attractive on the basis of
good value for good service.

The strategic move toward a shared captive center model requires the involvement of the parent firm. The captive center will have to be more independent and apply a profit center approach to ensure that its growth strategy is realistic. However, the parent firm should be aware of this change program and invest in resources and capital to ensure stability as the captive center shifts from one mode of operation to another. Our research shows that such rapid growth might raise concerns in the parent firm, as the captive center is often perceived to be a service center, not an entrepreneurial venture. Concerns about the magnitude of the investment over time and the long-term objectives of the offshore asset may drive the parent firm's executives to oppose such a change. However, as the GlobalAirline case shows, a shared captive center that is managed properly can eventually return the investment made by the parent firm and become both a successful service center and a smart investment.

The second driver is about becoming a center of excellence in a particular business process. While increasing scale, the shared captive center should develop its learning capabilities to understand the market, its clients and their needs, and the products and services that dominate the market at the time. Shared captive centers can learn by setting up partnerships and alliances and working closely with their clients. For example, according to the BTO procurement manager, ITConsulting chose to set up partnerships with large firms to take advantage of "the different opportunities of building upscale knowledge in many other areas of the business."

Working closely with the parent firm can also be beneficial in the early stages of expansion. The parent firm can be instrumental in attracting customers, sharing contacts with the captive centers, and offering marketing and sales channels across the globe. According to the BTO procurement manager of ITConsulting, "Of course, you can understand and learn how our tools work, but not so many companies can have the presence of ITConsulting."

Clearly, by developing scale and becoming a center of excellence for a particular business process, the shared captive center can become an attractive acquisition by a local vendor or a private equity firm. For example, the venture capital firm interested in buying GlobalAirline's captive center attributed its interest to the fact that "the captive center has already established a leading position in the business process outsourcing segment in India."[8] Other experts have concurred with this observation, claiming that the main reason to develop a captive center is that the parent firm can hedge better when the captive center is sold.

### The Key Challenges for a Shared Captive Center: Relationships with the Parent Firm and Developing New Capabilities

Because becoming a service provider to external clients is a major change for the captive center, multiple challenges can surface during the transition, as well as with regard to the relationships with the parent firm. One major concern is the extent of autonomy that the captive center can maintain during the change process, as well as the extent of investment needed in order to ensure uninterrupted service to the parent.

Going beyond these strategic and operational concerns, another major challenge the captive center will face is to develop its own marketing and sales capabilities offshore. As a center used to focusing on servicing the parent firm, the captive center will need to ramp up sales and marketing capabilities relatively quickly in order to generate revenues, secure its autonomy, and ensure that existing clients are not affected by the speedy growth trend.

Finally, there is always a risk that by acquiring external clients, the captive center will share proprietary information with the parent firm's competitors. This brings to fore the challenges that the captive center will face when managing its relationships with the parent firm during this evolutionary path.

### Shared Captive Center: How to Cope with These Challenges

Our research shows that the parent firm has a critical influence on the captive center's ability to transform into a shared model. Without its support and without joint strategic planning of the captive's growth path, the captive center is bound to fail. Therefore, the captive center's top team should start this journey by consulting with the parent firm's top team about the revisited business plan and the business case for change. In particular, the business case should stress how the captive center plans to compete with established local vendors and what areas of business process specialization will be attractive to develop from a short-term and long-term standpoint. The discussions with the parent firm's top management should revolve around two scenarios: the parent firm maintains ownership of the growing captive center and therefore expects to see profits growing on a year-by-year basis, and the parent firm would consider divesting the captive center, having achieved certain growth targets. In this latter situation, the captive center should focus on growth and scale rather than margins and profits to attract potential buyers.

## Capabilities That a Shared Captive Center Should Develop

Developing new capabilities, particularly in the area of sales and marketing, requires an investment in resources (see figure 11.3). A clear plan should be developed with the help of the parent firm to ensure the captive center can use the parent firm's sales and marketing channels and can recruit specialists with the required domain knowledge of the captive center's specialization areas.

As the captive center becomes a sophisticated vendor, the business unit will develop advanced vendor sourcing capabilities. While sourcing management capabilities and governance capabilities are taken for granted, we pose program management as a capability that the captive center will need to develop to ensure that learning across various outsourcing projects is facilitated. We also expect the captive center to gain business development capabilities to ensure that partnerships and alliances are set with local vendors and strategic partners to enhance learning about the markets, the potential clientele base, and appealing products and services.

Additional capabilities should consist of focusing on innovation and integration with the parent firm. As the captive center acquires additional clients and its revenue stream steadily grows, the top management team will need to tighten its relationships with the parent firm and raise awareness across the global firm regarding its activities and solutions to secure support from the parent firm and seek opportunities to introduce the innovations and solutions originating within the captive center to the parent firm. We also see a major role for the captive center in developing an innovative line of services around its areas of specialization as its engagements with clients intensify and understanding of its market needs grows (table 11.4).

**Table 11.4**
Capabilities for shared captive centers

| Necessary capabilities | Additional capabilities |
| --- | --- |
| Sourcing management (external clients) | Integration and coordination (with parent firm) |
| Sales and marketing | |
| Business development | Innovation management |
| Governance (external clients and parent firm) | |
| Program management | |

> *Drivers for shared captive centers*   Reduce the cost of a unit processed offshore; increase scale; specialize and become a center of excellence
>
> *Shared captive center challenges*   Getting support from the parent firm and rapidly ramping up sales and marketing capabilities
>
> *Coping strategies*   Revise the business plan; work out the business case for two scenarios: maintaining ownership and divesting captive center; coordinate marketing efforts through the parent firm but also build expertise offshore
>
> *Developed capabilities*   Sourcing management; sales and marketing; business development; governance and program management

## Evolving into a Divested Captive Center

When a captive center is divested, the parent firm takes the lead with regard to the ownership structure, the services to be divested, and the continuity of the service following completion of the transaction. Our research shows that a captive center is more likely to be divested successfully when it has built large-scale operations and has developed an area of specialty that is underdeveloped in the local market. These two factors will likely make the captive center attractive for acquisition by a local vendor looking to extend its service portfolio in line with the services offered by the captive center. Therefore, the evolutionary path expected for the divested captive center should include a hybrid and shared components to ensure that sufficient scale has been developed and that the captive center is running efficiently.

Nonetheless, as the AmeriBank case shows, not all captive centers are divested having followed these stages in their evolutionary path, simply because the decision to divest the captive center, taken by the parent firm, does not always consider the maturity, growth potential, and strategic role of the captive center (as depicted in figure 11.4). As we have seen during the financial crisis beginning in 2008, parent

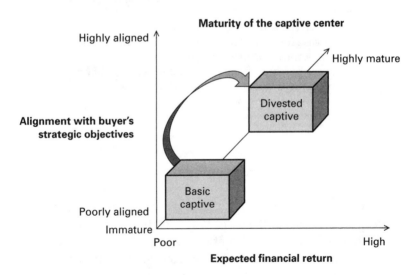

**Figure 11.4**
Why divest? Key decision-making aspects the parent firm should consider

firms divested their captive center to raise cash quickly and improve their financial strength.

Attracting investors is becoming a challenging task for parent firms globally. Recent evidence shows that about 60 percent of captive centers are in financial difficulty, and the growing pains experienced by private equity firms trying to raise money for investments during the financial crisis make it even more difficult for parent firms attract potential buyers. Therefore, parent firms can follow several tactics to improve the marketability of their captive centers. Some, in particular small firms, can try to attract potential buyers by setting up joint ventures to develop products or services with them. This was the case with the divestment of the Consumer-Goods captive center. Others, in most cases large multinationals that work with many vendors, can enhance their strategic partnerships with some local vendors that provide them outsourcing services in order to expose the vendors to the line of services the captive center offers and present such an investment as part of the broad relationship between the parties.

There is also the issue of the parent firm's ownership. Some parent firms prefer to sell off a majority stake in the captive center, and others prefer to maintain a controlling position over the captive. Captive centers that have reached a high maturity level in terms of their service and processes are more likely to be candidates for a majority divestment because the parent firm can assume that the level of service provided by the new owner of the captive center will be on par with their own standards. In fact, in such situations the parent firm will expect the service levels to improve as the acquired captive center is likely to grow, attract additional clients, learn, improve its practices, and provided better service. Some parent firms maintain a majority stake in the captive center; they view the business processes as critical to their success, or they are concerned with the quality of the service after the acquisition and would like to maintain control. Another reason to divest a small majority stake of the captive center is that the parent firm expects the acquiring party to make a significant investment in the captive center and anticipates that the remaining stake will appreciate over time. This was the case with GlobalAirline.

Finally, the parent firm should give great consideration to choosing the most appropriate divesting partner. Although the focus of most parent firms is on the valuation of the captive center, it is no less important to understand whether the acquiring party has the vision and ability to ensure the same or better service levels. Clearly both parent firm and captive center face major challenges in sailing through this change process.

### The Key Challenges for Divested Captive Center

### Choosing the Best Buyer, Maintaining Service Levels, and Preparing to Become a Sophisticated Outsourcing Consumer

The challenges prior to and during the divestment phase relate to the selection of the buyer and the ability to ensure existing or better service levels. Both parent firm and captive center will face these challenges. The key challenge when selecting the buyer is to find a fit between the strategic vision of the buyer for the captive center (e.g., which line of services will be further developed, which will be consolidated with exiting services, which services will be migrated to another service center, and which will be terminated) and the future needs of the parent firm in terms of outsourcing.

In our research, we observed that the buying party sets an agenda that is not always in the selling party's best interest. For example, some local vendors have been known to acquire captive centers only to integrate them later into existing service centers simply to increase scale and eliminate duplication of resources. Such a tactic may result in higher savings for the clients in the long term; however, this often results in interrupted service during the integration period. Maintaining high service levels is another challenge for the parent firm and the divested captive center. Some parent firms believe that the service standards on which the captive center has been established will be maintained by the new owner, while other parent firms attempt to mitigate the risk of losing control by setting up hundreds of service level agreements (SLAs). A good example of the latter is the GlobalAirline case, in which over one hundred new SLAs were put in place between the airline and the captive center as part of the contract to ensure continuity of service and information exchange after the transition. While SLAs may serve as a mitigation vehicle, they do not necessarily ensure the delivery of high-quality service. As the captive center goes through changes after the acquisition (e.g., changes in the management team, integration of services, shift in market focus in order to support growth), there could be an impact on the service that the captive center provides. These challenges require the captive center and the parent firm to consider together some mitigating strategies to ensure a smooth transition.

In the end, once the captive center has been divested, the parent firm is also changing its status from an internal consumer of services provided by the captive center to an external client that consumes outsourcing services from the vendor, formerly the captive center. Therefore, preparing the parent firm to act as a sophisticated player and ensuring that the captive center retains best practices as a vendor are key challenges for the parent firm. Often the acquiring firm will introduce change programs, or some key personnel will leave following the acquisition, which may likely result in the erosion of the sourcing capability developed within the captive center.

### Divested Captive Center: How to Cope with These Challenges

The journey to divest a captive center has to start with the parent firm's preparing the business unit for divestment and with a thorough audit regarding the parent firm's existing and future business needs in order to assess whether the captive center will be able to meet the parent firm's needs under the new ownership. During this audit, the parent firm should be able to answer some important questions: What services should have been provided by the captive center in the short and long terms? Which services provided by the captive center were in need of improvements? Should we not receive high-quality service from the captive center under the new ownership, what alternatives are there? Can we back-source these services?

Having answered these questions, the parent firm should develop a plan in search of a suitable buyer. It should seek to safeguard its assets and resources by either holding to a 51 percent stake in the captive center or negotiating an acquisition agreement that minimizes changes, at least in short term. For example, the parent firm should work with the acquiring party to offer key personnel a career path within the captive center under the new management. Pride and organizational culture should also be carefully addressed by both the parent firm and the acquiring party to ensure that staff do not become unmotivated and disengaged because of the change of ownership. Such tactics will also improve the retention of sourcing capabilities within the captive center, as it will switch status from being an internal service provider to becoming a third-party service provider.

The parent firm should take advantage of this change and consider the agility that the outsourcing relationships could offer if they are managed properly. For example, following the divestment of the captive center, the parent firm can benefit from the vendor's ability to scale operations up or down in line with market trends without having to engage in hiring.

## What Capabilities a Divested Captive Center/and Parent Firm Should Develop

While in most cases the parent firm takes the lead with regard to the actual divestment process, the captive center is by no means free of the challenges described. Certain capabilities should be developed within the captive center and in cooperation with the parent firm (table 11.5). These capabilities might have already been developed depending on the course of the captive center's development.

In particular, the strategic planning of the parent firm's service needs in the short and long terms should be developed in conjunction with the strategic planning of the captive center. The captive center's top team should be part of the

**Table 11.5**
Capabilities for divested captive centers

| Necessary capabilities | Additional capabilities |
| --- | --- |
| Strategic planning<br>Contract management<br>Talent management | Various capabilities will be developed depending on the changes introduced in the captive center following its divestment. |

strategic planning concerning its existing services and those to be purchased from it in the future. Contract management within the captive center and at the parent firm should be strengthened to ensure that both parties have a well-prepared outsourcing arrangement following the divestment of the captive center.

---

*Drivers to divest a captive center*   Financial incentives; focus on core activities; exiting a market

*Divesting challenges*   Choosing the right buyer; maintaining the same or better service levels; learning to become a sophisticated consumer of outsourcing products

*Coping strategies*   Perform a business requirements audit; perform a captive center performance audit; develop strong client and vendor capabilities

*Capabilities*   Strategic planning; contract management; talent management

---

**Toward a Generic Framework of Captive Center Strategies**

Our research shows that executives of multinationals have been pondering the future of their captive centers. The cases reported in this book also demonstrate the often ad hoc approach taken by executives regarding the strategic path of the captive center. Some firms divest their captive center simply because they need the capital or because of their inability to fix whatever problems they see in the captive center. Many embark on the captive center journey without being aware of the strategic options available and therefore miss important opportunities to develop the entity into a profit center and a source of innovation. With over $1.7

trillion allocated to back office operations every year by multinationals and as the offshoring market grows 5 percent annually, more and more firms will be considering the captive center option for business processes in different regions. We therefore now turn to the final question we address in this book: *Based on what criteria can executives make an informed decision regarding the evolutionary path of their captive center?*

Based on the extensive research we conducted over the past ten years into sourcing arrangements, country attractiveness, and captive centers, we see two necessary factors that a multinational should consider when embarking on the captive center journey: the parent firm's strategic intent and the local market conditions in the offshore location (figure 11.5). The concept of strategic intent can be translated into two aspects: cost advantage and growth opportunities. Local market conditions in the offshore location refer to the degree to which the local market in the offshore location is either developed or underdeveloped in terms of the demand for the services that the captive center offers. Underdeveloped markets mean a low demand for the captive center's services, and therefore we assume a small number of local vendors with little competition among them. A developed market in the offshore location represents high demand by local firms and a high number of innovative competitors.

The starting point for most multinationals is the decision to set up a captive center from scratch or acquire a local firm that specializes in providing outsourcing services. Multinationals that have arrived at a decision to set up a captive center in an offshore location should start by determining their strategic intent in setting up a captive center: Is it cost driven, or is it to exploit growth opportunities? They also should study the local market by trying to answer the

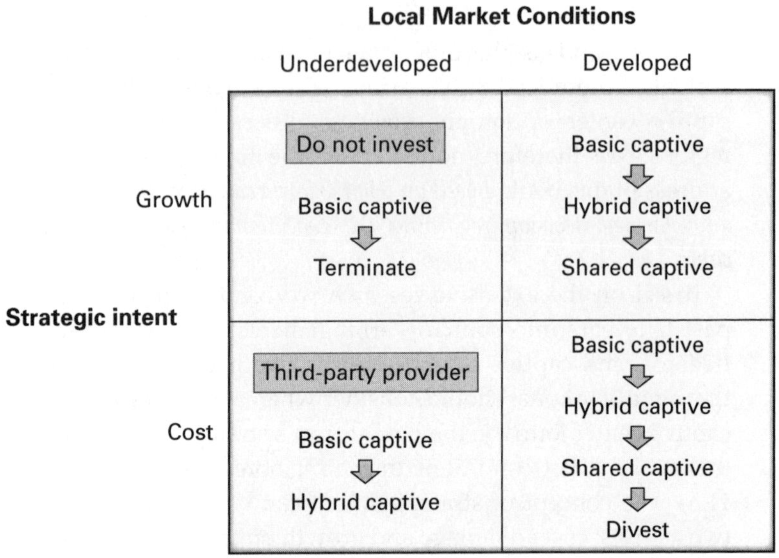

**Local Market Conditions**

| | Underdeveloped | Developed |
|---|---|---|
| **Growth** | Do not invest<br><br>Basic captive<br>⬇<br>Terminate | Basic captive<br>⬇<br>Hybrid captive<br>⬇<br>Shared captive |
| **Cost** | Third-party provider<br><br>Basic captive<br>⬇<br>Hybrid captive | Basic captive<br>⬇<br>Hybrid captive<br>⬇<br>Shared captive<br>⬇<br>Divest |

**Strategic intent**

**Figure 11.5**
Strategic captive options: Strategic intent and local conditions

following question: Are there numerous sophisticated vendors that specialize in the same or neighboring areas of business process services that the captive center should provide to the parent firm?

If they are cost driven and the market is underdeveloped, we advise firms to consider an outsourcing arrangement with a third-party service provider instead of setting up their own captive center. Underdeveloped markets for outsourcing services will lack skilled employees, a problem that will become a major challenge for the captive center when it needs to recruit the talent required to maintain service levels on par with the service provided onshore. Similarly, an underdeveloped market of outsourcing services in the offshore location will limit the captive center opportunities to grow and set up partnerships with local vendors. However, if the multinational decides to set up a captive center regardless of these challenges due to the potential cost savings that a captive center can offer, we advise that the parent firm and the captive center maintain a basic captive center model.

If the strategic intent is to exploit growth opportunities and the country selection is in an underdeveloped local market, we advise executives not to invest in a captive center. The conditions within which the captive center will operate (lack of demand from external local clients, lack of skills, and lack of competition to drive innovation) will not support the center's growth plans. An example comes from some recent reports about emerging offshoring destinations in the Middle East claiming that several of those countries offer advanced engineering and multilingual skills, as well as a service mentality that make them attractive locations to set up a captive center to service the entire Middle East. Our research found that only Egypt has developed both sufficient engineering and language skills to be considered a hub for multinationals wishing to service the entire region. Captive centers that operate in underdeveloped market conditions with the strategic intention to grow should be shut down.

A multinational considering setting up a captive center in a developed market with a strategic growth intention should take advantage of the range of opportunities to improve the captive center operations by moving from a basic to a hybrid and to a shared captive center over time. Considering that the local market is populated with numerous vendors, the captive center should exploit opportunities to outsource some of its activities in order to become more efficient and free up talent to focus on higher-level activities. At the same time, the captive center should attract external clients to increase scale, learn about markets and needs, and pursue innovation. The captive center can partner with local vendors and work closely with the parent firm to attract new clients.

A strategic intent focusing on achieving costs saving by setting up a captive center in a developed local market is another opportunity to exploit local market conditions. Over time, such a center should evolve into a hybrid captive center, having outsourced some of its noncore activities to local vendors. Developing scale should become a key objective for the captive center, and the parent firm should consider its strategic role in both the short and long terms. The parent firm can maintain full ownership of the captive center and benefit from the costs savings offered by the captive center as the scale of transactions processed offshore increases. Or the parent firm could consider divesting the captive center (the entire entity or portions of it) in order to focus on its core activities while becoming a client of the captive center after it is sold.

There is no one best method for pursuing a captive center strategy. A best-fit strategy depends on the strategic goals of the parent company, as well as the environment in which the captive center operates. Furthermore, captive centers should not be treated as service centers. They should be viewed as business units that can offer growth opportunities when they are carefully aligned with the multinational's overall global strategy.

### Epilogue

On June 30 , 2009, Stephanie Overby, a well-respected journalist, published an article in *CIO* announcing the demise of the offshore captive center.[9] In this book, I argue that the destiny of captive centers is far from death. If anything, the captive center as a concept is in its infancy, and as a child it is learning to adapt and react to the environment. In addition, its development depends on its relationship with the parent firm. Resources, commitment, and nurturing are among the critical enablers that the parent firm can offer its captive center to support its growth and, eventually, its independence in the long term.

Of course, a parent firm can devote resources and management attention and eventually realize that its captive center is an unwanted child. I accept that many captive centers struggle, and some are going through near-death experiences; however, in many of the cases, the reason for this unfortunate fate is two pitfalls in management's planning approach. The first drawback is the lack of a thorough examination of the very simple question: Do we want this child, and why? The second is the lack of an ongoing debate and eventually a decision within the parent firm about what it would like this child to be (as opposed to the discourse in most firms about what the captive center is).

Going through the infancy years with support, nurturing, and clear direction will allow the captive center to develop its identity, assume responsibility, and contribute back to the parent firm to the point when it is time to spread its wings and fly away.

# Notes

## Chapter 1

1. S. Overby, "Outsourcing: The Demise of the Offshore Captive Center," *CIO*, June 30, 2009, available at http://www.cio.com/article/496322/Outsourcing_The_Demise_of_the_Offshore_Captive_Center?page=1&taxonomyId=3195.

2. Dell, "Dell Inc. Sells El Salvador Contact Center to Stream Global Services, Inc.," October 15, 2008, available at http://www.dell.com/content/topics/global.aspx/corp/pressoffice/en/2008/2008_10_15_rr_001?c=us&l=en.

3. Overby, "Outsourcing."

4. T. Hutchens, "Dell Sells Refurbishing Plant in Lebanon," *Nashville Business Journal*, July 16, 2009, available at http://nashville.bizjournals.com/nashville/stories/2009/07/13/daily39.html.

5. M. A. Chanchani, "Exl Acquires American Express Captive for $30 M," *VCCircle*, November 7, 2009, available at http://www.vccircle.com/500/news/exl-acquires-american-express-captive-for-30m.

6. Overby, "Outsourcing."

7. K. Goolsby, "Part I–Trends in Offshore Captive Services Centers: Interview of Everest Research Institute's Salil Dani," *Outsourcing Buzz Blog*, February 10, 2010, available at http://www.outsourcing-buzz-blog.com/2010/02/interview_of_ev.html.

8. K. Goolsby, "Part II–Trends in Offshore Outsourced Services: Interview of Salil Dani, Everest Research Institute," *Outsourcing Buzz Blog*, February

10, 2010, available at http://www.outsourcing-buzz-blog.com/2010/02/interview_of_sa.html.

9. "Everest Q1 Report: Outsourcing Market Signals Steady Economic Recovery," *Business Wire*, May 5, 2010, available at http://www.forbes.com/feeds/businesswire/2010/05/05/businesswire139198560.html.

10. S. J. Palmisano, "The Globally Integrated Enterprise," *Foreign Affairs* 85, no. 3 (2006): 127–136.

11. J. Lampel and A. Bhalla, "Embracing Realism and Recognizing Choice in IT Offshoring Initiatives," *Business Horizons* 51 (2008): 429–440.

12. R. Aron, "Business Processes Are Moving from the West to Other Parts of the World," *Knowledge@Wharton*, November 18, 2002, available at http://knowledge.wharton.upenn.edu/article.cfm?articleid=630.

13. T. L. Friedman, *The World Is Flat: A Brief History of the Twenty-First Century* (New York: Farrar, Straus and Giroux, 2005).

14. A. Bierce, S. Spohr, and R. Shah, "Captive No More," *Executive Agenda* 7, no. 2 (2004), 5–10.

15. S. Ante, "Shifting Work Offshore? Outsourcer Beware," *BusinessWeek* January 12, 2004, available at http://www.businessweek.com/magazine/content/04_02/b3865028.htm.

16. P. McDougall, "Offshoring Will Remain Strong for India's Big Four," *Information Week Online*, May 24, 2004, available at http://www.informationweek.com/showArticle.jhtml?articleID=20900333&fb=20040615_software.

17. P. Maskell, T. Pedersen, B. Petersen and J. Dick-Neilsen, *Learning Paths to Offshore Outsourcing: From Cost Reduction to Knowledge Seeking* (Copenhagen, Denmark: Copenhagen Business School, 2006).

18. The following reading provides more information about these aspects: E. Carmel and P. Tija, *Offshoring Information Technology* (Cambridge: Cambridge University Press, 2005).

19. I. Oshri, J. Kotlarsky, J. W. Rottman, and L .P. Willcocks , "A Review of Trends in Global Sourcing of Services," *Information Technology and People* 22, no. 3 (2009): 192–201.

20. "Siemens CEO Klaus Kleinfeld: Nobody's Perfect But a Team Can Be," (April 19, 2006) *Knowledge@Wharton*, available at http://knowledge.wharton.upen.edu/article.cfm?articleid-1447

21. N. Shivapriya, "Captive BPO Centers Begin to Pay Off," (September 28, 2007) *India Times*, available at http://economictimes.indiatimes.com/ InfoTech/ITeS/Captive_BPO_centers_begin_to_pay_off/articleshow/ 2402877.cms

22. Everest Research Institute, *Market Vista: Q2 2008* (Dallas, TX: Everest Research Institute, 2008).

23. Carmel and Tija, *Offshoring Information Technology*.

24. D. Farrell, "Offshoring: Value Creation through Economic Change," *Journal of Management Studies* 42 (2005): 675–682.

25. G. Erber and A. Sayed-Ahmed, "Offshore Outsourcing: A Global Shift in the Present," *IT Industry Intereconomics* 40, no. 2 (2005): 100–112. M. Tafti, "Risk Factors Associated with Offshore IT Outsourcing," *Industrial Management and Data Systems* 105, no. 5 (2005): 549–560.

26. Carmel and Tija, *Offshoring Information Technology*.

27. A. Y. Lewin and C. Peeters, "Offshoring Work: Business Hype or the Onset of Fundamental Transformation?" *Long Range Planning* 39 (2006): 221–239.

28. I. Oshri, J. Kotlarsky, and C. M. Liew, "Four Strategies for 'Offshore' Captive Centers," *Wall Street Journal*, May 12, 2008, R4.

29. I. Oshri et al., "Trends in Global Sourcing."

30. Lampel and Bhalla, "Embracing Realism and Recognizing Choice in IT Offshoring Initiatives."

**Chapter 2**

1. M. Subramanian and B. Atri, "Captives in India: A Research Study," *Infosys* (2006), available at http://www.infosys.com/global-sourcing/ white-papers/captives-research-v2.pdf.

2. I. Oshri, J. Kotlarsky, J. W. Rottman, and L. P. Willcocks, "Global Outsourcing: Recent Trends and Issues," *Information Technology and People* 22, no.3 (2009): 192–200.

3. N. Levina, "In or Out in an Offshore Context: The Choice between Captive Centers and Third-Party Vendors," *Cutter IT Journal* (2006): 24–28, available at http://www.cutter.com/content/itjournal/fulltext/2006/12/ itj0612d.html.

4. Oshri, Kotlarsky, Rottman, and Willcocks, "Global Outsourcing."

5. I. Oshri, J. Kotlarsky, and L. Willcocks, *The Handbook of Global Outsourcing and Offshoring* (London: Palgrave, 2009).

6. P. Allery, *Tolley's Effective Outsourcing: Practice and Procedures* (Corydon: LexisNexis, 2004). P. Donlon and J. Kropp, "Offshore versus Onshore Outsourcing," *API Outsourcing* (2005), available at http://www.apifao.com/company/news15_offshore_vs_onshore.html.

7. R. Aron, "Why Corporations Pursue BPO [interview with Peter Bendor-Samuel, Founder and CEO of Everest Group, and James B. Quinn, professor of management emeritus at Dartmouth College]," *Knowledge@Wharton* (2004), available at http://knowledge.wharton.upenn.edu/article.cfm?articleid=860.

8. Allery, *Tolley's Effective Outsourcing*.

9. A. Vashistha and A. Vashistha, *The Offshore Nation-Strategies for Success in Global Outsourcing and Offshoring* (New York: McGraw-Hill, 2006).

10. L. Willcocks, C. Griffiths, and J. Kotlarsky, "Beyond BRIC. Offshoring in Non-BRIC Countries: Egypt—A New Growth Market" (London: LSE Outsourcing, 2009).

11. Oshri, Kotlarsky, and Willcocks, *The Handbook of Global Outsourcing and Offshoring*.

12. I. Hunter, *The Indian Offshore Advantage: How Offshoring Is Changing the Face of HR* (Aldershot: Gower House, 2006).

13. R. Gonzalez, J. Gasco, and J. Llopis, "Information Systems Offshore Outsourcing: A Descriptive Analysis," *Industrial Management and Data Systems* 106, no. 9 (2006): 1233–1248.

14. W. Van Acker, "Going Global: Strategies and Issues," *Automotive Design and Production* 118, no.11 (2006): 20.

15. J. Steele, "The Outlook on Outsourcing," *Wide Format Imaging* 15, no. 11 (2007): 16.

16. Aron, "Why Corporations Pursue BPO."

17. W. Rottman, "Successful Knowledge Transfer within Offshore Supplier Networks: A Case Study Exploring Social Capital in Strategic Alliances," *Journal of Information Technology* 23 (2008): 31–43.

18. P. W. Beamish and J. P. Killing, *Cooperative Strategies: European Perspectives* (San Francisco: New Lexington Press, 1997).

19. I. Oshri, J. Kotlarsky, and C. M. Liew, "Four Strategies for 'Offshore' Captive Centers," *Wall Street Journal,* May 12, 2008, R4.

20. Subramanian and Atri, "Captives in India."

21. "A Look at Captive Offshoring," *Offshoring Times* (2008), available at http://www.offshoringtimes.com/Pages/2008/offshore_news1889.html.

22. Subramanian and Atri, "Captives in India."

23. P. Mishra, "Outsourcing Sees Mix and Match with Captives, 3rd Party Vendors," *Wall Street Journal,* June 15, 2007, available at http://www.livemint.com/2007/06/15003046/Outsourcing-sees-mix-and-match.html.

24. Subramanian and Atri, "Captives in India."

25. Ibid.

26. J. P. Menezes, "Captive Centre Outsourcing Option Not So Captivating," *itbusiness.ca* (2007), available at http://www.itbusiness.ca/it/client/en/Home/News.asp?id=46300&bSearch=True.

27. Hunter, *The Indian Offshore Advantage;* Preston, "Lost in Migration"; and M. RajeevanM. Subramanian, P. Beligere, and R. Williams, *Research Study of Captives in India and China: A Majority of Parent Organizations Also Rely on Third-Party Relationships* (Bangalore: Infosys, 2007).

28. S. Vedala, "Ten Steps to Setting Up a Captive Offshore Service Centre," *Equaterra* (2008), available at http://www.equaterra.com/_filelib/FileCabinet/News/EquaTerra_Article_Setting_Up_Captive_Offshore_Svc_Ctr_Nov2007_3021EU.pdf?FileName=EquaTerra_Article_Setting_Up_Captive_Offshore_Svc_Ctr_Nov2007_3021EU.pdf.

29. Preston, "Lost in Migration."

30. Menezes, "Captive Centre Outsourcing Option Not So Captivating."

31. "Look at Captive Offshoring."

32. I. Oshri, J. Kotlarsky, and C. M. Liew, "Four Strategies for `Offshore' Captive Centers."

33. B. Ghosh and S. Iyer, "Future Bright for Captive Bpos," *Hindu Business Line* (2007), available at http://www.thehindubusinessline.com/ew/2007/10/01stories/2007100150100300.htm.

34. R. Aron, "Business Processes Are Moving from the West to Other Parts of the World," *Knowledge@Wharton* (2002), available at http://knowledge.wharton.upenn.edu/article.cfm?articleid=630.

35. S. Preston, "Being Busy Abroad Yourself Could Be Best," *Human Resource Management International Digest* 13, no.3 (2005): 13–14.

36. Ghosh and Iyer, "Future Bright for Captive Bpos."

37. D. Murali, "Life Cycle of a Captive BPO," *Hindu Business Line* (2005), available at http://www.thehindubusinessline.com/ew/2005/02/19/stories/2005091900300400.

38. "A Look at Captive Offshoring."

39. N. Athresh, "Captive Centres in India," *Globonomics* (2007), available at http://ecofin.wordpress.com/2007/05/17/captive-product-units/.

40. A. Mukherjee, "India May Soon Boot Out as a BPO-Perfect Nation" San Francisco: India Resource Center, 2007), available at http://www.indiaresource.org/news/2007/1040.html.

41. R. Aron, "The Little Start-Up That Could: A Conversation with Raman Roy, Father of Indian BPO—Part 2," *Knowledge@Wharton* (2003), available at http://knowledge.wharton.upenn.edu/articlepdf/794.pdf?CFID=14941363&CFTOKEN=93016593&jsessionid=a8309169a5987ee557dd62b4d12717e5b777.

42. S. Gibson, *IT* "Management-Indian Outsourcer WNS Readies IPO," *eWeek* (2006), available at http://www.accessmylibrary.com/coms2/summary_0286-16095602_ITM.

43. Ghosh and Iyer, "Future Bright for Captive BPOs."

44. Aron, 'Why Corporations Pursue BPO [interview with Peter Bendor-Samuel, Founder and CEO of Everest Group, and James B. Quinn, professor of management emeritus at Dartmouth College'.

45. A. Maheshwari, *The Offshore Captive Center Model* (Tucson: Eller College of Management, University of Arizona, 2005).

46. Ghosh and Iyer, "Future Bright for Captive BPOs."

47. Mukherjee, "India May Soon Boot Out as a BPO-Perfect Nation."

48. To learn more about virtual captive centers, see http://www.outsourcing-offshore.com/thought.html.

49. M. Bloch, S. Narayanan, and I. Seth, "Getting More Out of Offshoring the Finance Function," *McKinsey Quarterly* (2007): 1–6, available at http://www.conseroglobal.com/pdf/news_offshoring.pdf.

50. S. Overby, "Offshore Outsourcing: Can This Captive Center Be Saved?" *CIO* (2007), available at http://www.cio.com/article/152701/Offshore _Outsourcing_Can_This_Captive_Center_Be_Saved_.

51. T. Gold, *Outsourcing Software Development Offshore-Making it Work* (Boca Raton, FL: Auerbach Publications, 2004).

52. N. Kaka, "Running a Customer Service Center in India: An Interview with the Head of Operations for Dell India," *McKinseyonIT* (Summer 2006): 22–26.

53. R. Aron, "Why Corporations Pursue BPO" [interview with Peter Bendor-Samuel, Founder and CEO of Everest Group, and James B. Quinn, professor of management emeritus at Dartmouth College].

54. R. Jester, *Should You Spin Off Your IT and Become an External Service Provider?* Gartner Audio Teleconference (2005).

55. A. Hanson, "What Does the Reported Sale of Citigroup BPO Mean?" *TPI.net* (2007), available at http://www.tpi.net/pdf/pointofview/TPI _POV_Citibank_BPO.pdf.

56. D. Ross, "Captive Carve Outs" (Global Services: 2007), available at http://www.globalservicesmedia.com/content/general200709182883.asp.

57. M. Tejaswi, "Big Guns Opt Out of Citi BPO Deal," *Times of India* (2007), available at http://timesofindia.indiatimes.com/Big_guns_opt_out_of _Citi_BPO_deal/articleshow/2172373.cms.

58. "Captive BPO Arms Are Passed," *Times of India* (2007), available at http://it.tmcnet.com/news/2007/11/09/3084544.htm.

59. R. Martin, "India Retains the Offshore Outsourcing Crown," *Offshoring Times* (2007), available at http://www.offshoringtimes.com/Pages/2007/ offshore_news1839.html.

60. S. Preston, "Lost in Migration: Offshore Need Does Not Mean Outsourced," *Strategy and Leadership* 32, no.6 (2004): 32–36.

61. A.T. Kearney, *Making Offshore Decisions: A.T. Kearney's 2004 Offshore Location Attractiveness Index* (Chicago: A.T. Kearney: 2004).

## Chapter 3

1. L. P. Willcocks and M. Lacity, *The Practice of Outsourcing: From ITO to BPO and Offshoring* (London: Palgrave, 2009).

2. Ibid.

3. A. Reinhardt, "Angling to be the Next Bangalore," *Business Week* (January 30, 2006) available at http://www.businessweek.com/magazine/content/06_05/b3969409.htm.

4. J. Kotlarsky and I. Oshri, "Country Attractiveness for Offshoring and Offshore-Outsourcing: Additional Considerations," *Journal of Information Technology* 23, no.4, (2008): 228–231.

5. Willcocks and Lacity, *The Practice of Outsourcing*.

6. *The Black Book of Outsourcing: State of the Outsourcing Industry 2007* (Brown-Wilson Group New York, 2008), available at http://www.theblackbookofoutsourcing.com/.

7. Willcocks and Lacity, *The Practice of Outsourcing*.

8. *The Black Book of Outsourcing*.

9. E. Carmel, "The New Software Exporting Nations: Success Factors," *Electronic Journal on Information Systems in Developing Countries* 13, no. 4 (2003): 1–12. The eight factors are: government vision and policies, human capital, wages, quality of life, linkages between individuals and firms, technological infrastructure, capital, and some industry characteristics.

10. D. Farrell, "Smarter Offshoring," *Harvard Business Review* 84, no. 6 (2006): 85–92.

11. Ibid.

12. Everest Research Institute, *Market Vista: Q2 2008* (Dallas: Everest Research Group, 2008).

13. E. Carmel and P. Abbott, 'Why Nearshore Means That Distance Matters," *Communications of the ACM* 50, no. 10 (2007): 40–46.

14. A. Vashistha and I. Khan, *Top 50 Emerging Global Outsourcing Cities* (2008), available at http://www.globalservicesmedia.com/Userfiles/file/top50_eoc_report.pdf.

15. Farrell, "Smarter Offshoring."

**Chapter 4**

1. We investigated captive centers of both client firms and vendors (e.g., IBM). For vendors, we examined the role that global delivery centers play

in providing services to the vendor or external clients to determine whether they can be considered as captive centers.

2. I. Oshri, J. Kotlarsky, and C. Liew, "Four Offshore Captive Center Strategies for Offshore," *Wall Street Journal*, May 12, 2008.

3. M. Graf and S. M. Mudambi, "The Outsourcing of IT-Enabled Business Processes: A Conceptual Model of the Location Decision," *Journal of International Management* 11 (2005): 253–268.

4. Offshoring Research Network, "Software and Product Development Offshoring: Findings from ORN 2007/2008 Duke University" (2008), available at http://www.offshoring.guqua.duke.edu/community/index.html.

5. I. Oshri and J. Kotlarsky, "Realising the Real Benefits of Outsourcing: Seven Steps to Effective Outsourcing Measurement" (Warwick: Warwick Business School, 2009).

6. A.T. Kearney, "Offshoring for Long-Term Advantage: The 2007 A.T. Kearney Global Services Location Index" (Chicago: A.T. Kearney, 2007).

7. Jones Lang Lasalle, "India 30: Real Estate Opportunities in Tier III Cities," *Global Foresight* (2008).

8. NASSCOM-McKinsey, "NASSCOM-McKinsey Report 2005: Extending India's Leadership of the Global IT and BPO Industries" (Bangalore: NASSCOM-McKinsey, 2005).

9. A. McCue, "HSBC Ramps Up Indian Presence," *ZDNet Asia* (2006), available at http://www.zdnetasia.com/news/business/0,39044229,61970344,00.htm.

10. Tholons, "Top 50 Emerging Outsourcing Destinations 2008" (New York: Tholons, 2008).

11. See S. Overby, "Global Outsourcing Guide," in *Offshore Outsourcing Guide* (2006), available at http://www.cio.com/archive/071506/2006_global_outsourcing_guide.pdf.

12. Jones Lang Lasalle, "India 30."

13. D. Hoch, M. Kwiecinski, and P. Peters, "The Overlooked Potential for Outsourcing in Eastern Europe," *McKinseyonIT* (Winter 2006), available at http://www.mckinsey.com/clientservice/bto/pointofview/pdf/MoIT10_eastern_euro.pdf.

14. Citigroup Global Service Centers in Budapest, *Citibank Press Room*, November 24, 2006, available at https://www.citibank.hu/hungary/homepage/sajtoszoba/hirek/061124_e.htm.

15. Zinnov Consultancy Management, "Strategic Guide on Indian R&D Centers 2008" (2008), available at http://www.zinnov.com/.

16. A.T. Kearney, "Offshoring for Long-Term Advantage: The 2009 A.T. Kearney Global Services Location Index" (Chicago: A.T. Kearney, 2009).

**Chapter 5**

1. This case is based on the work of Anne Katrin Debusmann, a Rotterdam School of Management CEMS graduate, under the supervision of the author.

**Chapter 6**

This case is based on the work of Anne Katrin Debusmann, a Rotterdam School of Management CEMS graduate, under the supervision of the author.

**Chapter 7**

This case is based on the work of Anne Katrin Debusmann, a Rotterdam School of Management CEMS graduate, under the supervision of the author.

1. D. Filkins, article, *Indian Embassy*, April 6, 2000.

2. Thomson Reuters, article, *Reuters News*, October 23, 2001.

3. *Financial Times*, article, April 4, 2002.

4. Thompson Reuters, October 23, 2001.

5. *Business Standard*, article, April 5, 2002.

6. *eFinancial News*, article, April 4, 2002.

7. The Times of India Group, Article, *Economic Times*, April 30, 2002.

8. Asia Pacific Communications Limited, Article, *Asia Private Equity Review*, April 1, 2002.

9. *Global Outsourcer*, press release, April 28, 2003.

10. Hackett Group, report (2008).

11. *Knowledge@Wharton*, article, January 14, 2005.

12. Seeking Alpha, article, *Financial Stocks: Insurance* (2008).

## Chapter 8

This case is based on the work of Anne Katrin Debusmann, a Rotterdam School of Management CEMS graduate, under the supervision of the author.

1. *InformationWeek,* article, October 8, 2008.

2. AmeriBank, *Annual Report 2006–2007* (2007), available at AmeriBank Web site

3. Press Trust of India Limited, article, November 9, 2006.

4. *Hindu Business Line,* article, November 9, 2006.

5. P. Moreira, article, *TheDeal.com* (April 2008).

6. Voxant FD Wire, conference call October 8, 2008.

7. *InformationWeek,* article, October 8, 2008.

8. *eBanking&Payment News,* article, November 5, 2008.

9. Voxant FD Wire, conference call.

10. *International Herald Tribune,* article, October 9, 2008.

11. Workforce Management, article, May 19, 2008.

12. Voxant FD Wire, conference call.

## Chapter 9

This case is based on the work of Anne Katrin Debusmann, a Rotterdam School of Management CEMS graduate, under the supervision of the author.

## Chapter 10

This case is based on the work of Claudio Hasler, a Rotterdam School of Management CEMS graduate, under the supervision of the author.

1. Markham (Canada), Poughkeepsie (United States), Rio, North Harbour (United Kingdom), Stuttgart (Germany), Bordeaux (France), Shanghai (China), Tokyo (Japan), and Melbourne (Australia).

2. Bangalore for the United States, Canada, Australia and New Zealand, and ASEAN; Shanghai for China, Taiwan, Hong Kong, Korea, and Japan; Budapest for Europe, the Middle East, and Africa and for Latin America.

3. Vice president is a high position within the company; The two vice presidents noted in the text are responsible for several thousand employees. This demonstrates the importance assigned to the task of the location assessment.

4. The SPP manager reported that out of roughly 300 people, only about 120 joined the all-hands meeting. The informational sessions had about 20 participants each.

5. According to the Nordic team manager, BTO faced problems from the beginning. People were rather negative about the positions. However, when BTO started producing good results, attitudes changed for the better.

**Chapter 11**

1. M. Subramanian and B. Atri, "Captives in India: A Research Study," *Infosys* (2006), available at http://www.infosys.com/global-sourcing/white-papers/captives-research-v2.pdf.

2. F. W. McFarlan and R. I. Nolan, "How to Manage an IT Outsourcing Alliance," *Sloan Management Review* (Winter 2005), 9–23.

3. A. Vashistha and A. Vashistha, *The Offshore Nation-Strategies for Success in Global Outsourcing and Offshoring* (New York: McGraw-Hill, 2006).

4. *Hindu Business Line,* Article (2001).

5. R. Aron, "Why Corporations Pursue BPO," *Knowledge@Warton* (2004).

6. J. Kotlarsky and I. Oshri, "Country Attractiveness for Offshoring and Offshore-Outsourcing," *Journal of Information Technology* 23, no. 4 (2008): 228–231.

7. P. Nair, "The Risk and Benefits of Outsourcing," *Pharma-Mag*, July 8, 2008, 28–30.

8. *Business Standard,* Article, (April 5, 2002).

9. See http://www.cio.com/article/496322/Outsourcing_The_Demise_of_the_Offshore_Captive_Center.

# References

A.T. Kearney. 2004. *Making offshore decisions: A.T. Kearney's 2004 offshore location attractiveness index*. Chicago: A.T. Kearney. Retrieved from http://www.atkearney.com/images/global/pdf/Making_offshore_s.pdf.

A.T. Kearney. 2007. *Offshoring for long-term advantage: The 2007 A.T. Kearney Global Services Location Index*. Chicago: A.T. Kearney. Retrieved from http://www.atkearney.com/res/shared/pdf/GSLI_2007.pdf.

A.T. Kearney. 2009. *Global Services Location Index*. Chicago: A. T. Kearney. Retrieved from http://www.atkearney.com/index.php/Publications/global-services-location-index-gsli-2009-report.html.

Ante, S. January 12, 2004. Shifting work offshore? Outsourcer beware. *BusinessWeek*. Retrieved from http://www.businessweek.com/magazine/content/04_02/b3865028.htm.

Aron, R. 2002, November 18. Business processes are moving from the West to other parts of the world. *Knowledge@Wharton*. Retrieved from http://knowledge.wharton.upenn.edu/article.cfm?articleid=630.

Aron, R. 2003. The little start-up that could: A conversation with Raman Roy, father of Indian BPO—Part 2. *Knowledge@Wharton*. Retrieved from http://knowledge.wharton.upenn.edu/articlepdf/794.pdf?CFID=14941363.&CFTOKEN=93016593&jsessionid=a8309169a5987ee557dd62b4d12717e5b777.

Aron, R. 2004, March 24. Why corporations pursue BPO [Interview with Peter Bendor-Samuel, founder and CEO of Everest Group, and James B. Quinn, professor of management emeritus at Dartmouth College]. *Knowledge@Wharton*. Retrieved from http://knowledge.wharton.upenn.edu/article.cfm?articleid=860.

Aron, R. 2005. How some BPO providers seek to build and protect their turf. *Knowledge@Wharton.* Retrieved from http://knowledge.wharton.upenn .edu/article.cfm?articleid=1101.

As the BPO business grows, there's a greater focus on metrics and measurement. 2005. *Knowledge@Wharton.* Retrieved from http://knowledge .wharton.upenn.edu/article.cfm?articleid=1102.

Athresh, N. 2007, May 17. Captive centres in India [Blog]. http://ecofin .wordpress.com/2007/05/17/captive-product-units/.

Baily, M., and R. Lawrence. 2004. What happened to the great U.S. job machine? The role of trade and electronic offshoring. *Brookings Papers on Economic Activity* 2:271–282. Retrieved from http://www.hks.harvard.edu/ fs/rlawrence/BPEA%20Baily-Lawr%20Oct%208%20clean.pdf.

Bhargava, N. 2006. Turning Indian outsourcing units into cash. *Offshoring-Times.* Retrieved from http://www.offshoringtimes.com/Pages/2006/ BPO_news1342.html.

Bierce, A., S. Spohr, and R. Shah. 2004. Captive no more. *Executive Agenda* 7(2): 5–10. Retrieved from http://www.atkearney.com/images/global/ pdf/EA72_CaptiveNoMore_S.pdf.

Bivens, J. 2005, August 1. Truth and consequences of offshoring: Recent studies overstate the benefits and ignore the costs to American workers. Economic Policy Institute briefing paper 155. Retrieved from http:// www.epi.org/publications/entry/bp155/.

Bloch, M., S. Narayanan, and I. Seth. April 2007. Getting more out of offshoring the finance function. *McKinsey Quarterly*, 1–6. Retrieved from http:// www.conseroglobal.com/pdf/news_offshoring.pdf.

BPO growing amid moderate satisfaction. 2005. *Managing Offshore.* Retrieved from http://www.equaterra.com/newsletters/ManagingOffshore_p20–24 _Jun05.pdf.

Captive BPO arms are passed. 2007. *Times of India.* Retrieved from http:// it.tmcnet.com/news/2007/11/09/3084544.htm.

The captive vendor model shift: Stake offloading by financial services firms. 2007, May 28. Retrieved from http://www.valuenotes.com/VNTeam/ vn_investfin_28May07.asp?ArtCd=109445&Cat=I&Id=14.

Carmel, E., and P. Tija. 2005. *Offshoring information technology.* Cambridge: Cambridge University Press.

Das, S. 2008, April 21. Half-filled or half empty? Retrieved from http:// dqindia.ciol.com/content/spotlight/2008/108042103.asp.

Donlon, P., and J. Kropp. 2005. Offshore versus onshore outsourcing. Retrieved from http://www.apifao.com/company/news15_offshore_vs _onshore.html.

Erber, G., and A. Sayed-Ahmed. 2005. Offshore outsourcing: A global shift in the present. *IT Industry. Inter Economics* 40 (2):100–112.

Everest Research Institute. 2008. *Market Vista: Q2 2008* (No. ERI-2008–8-R-0264). Dallas: Everest Research Institute. Retrieved from http:// www.everestresearchinstitute.com/News/10272.

Farey-Jones, D. 2005, October 27. Abbey applauded for bringing call centre work back to UK. Retrieved from http://www.brandrepublic.com/ News/524441/Abbey-applauded-bringing-call-centre-work-back-UK.

Farrell, D. 2005. Offshoring: Value creation through economic change. *Journal of Management Studies* 42:675–682.

Friedman, T. L. 2005. *The world is flat: A brief history of the twenty-first century.* New York: Farrar, Straus and Giroux.

Ghosh, B., and S. Iyer. 2007. Future bright for captive BPOs. Retrieved from http://www.thehindubusinessline.com/ew/2007/10/01stories/ 2007100150100300.htm.

Gibson, S. 2006. IT management-Indian outsourcer WNS readies IPO. Retrieved from http://www.accessmylibrary.com/coms2/summary _0286–16095602_ITM.

Global Services. 2006. Wachovia puts new spin on BPO. Retrieved from http://www.itbusinessedge.com/topics/reader.aspx?oss=20770.

Gold, T. 2004. *Outsourcing software development offshore: Making it work.* Boca Raton, FL: Auerbach Publications.

Gonzalez, R., J. Gasco, and J. Llopis. 2006. Information systems offshore outsourcing: A descriptive analysis. *Industrial Management & Data Systems* 106 (9):1233–1248.

Gottschalk, P., and H. Solli-Saether. 2005. Critical success factors from IT outsourcing theories: An empirical study. *Industrial Management & Data Systems* 105 (6):685–702.

Graf, M., and S. M. Mudambi. 2005. The outsourcing of IT-enabled business processes: A conceptual model of the location decision. *Journal of International Management* 11:253–268.

Hoch, D., M. Kwiecinski, and P. Peters. 2006, Winter. The overlooked potential for outsourcing in Eastern Europe. *McKinsey on IT*, 19–21. Retrieved

from     http://www.mckinsey.com/clientservice/bto/pointofview/pdf/
MoIT10_eastern_euro.pdf.

Horn, J., D. Lovallo, and S. Viguerie. 2006. Learning to let go: Making better
exit decisions. *McKinsey Quarterly* (2):64–75.

Hunter, I. 2006. *The Indian offshore advantage: How offshoring is changing the
face of HR*. Aldershot: Gower House.

Indo-Italian Chamber of Commerce and Industry. 2006. *Report on ICT industry in India*. Mumbai: Indo Italian Chamber of Commerce and Industry.
Retrieved     from     http://www.ud.camcom.it/internazionaliz/int_iniz/
allegati%20india/ICT_report.pdf.

Jarvenpaa, S., and J. L. Mao. 2008. Operational capabilities development in
mediated offshore software services models. *Journal of Information Technology*
23:3–17.

Jester, R. 2005, November 3. Should you spin off your IT and become an
external service provider? Teleconference presentation. Retrieved from
http://www.gartner.com/teleconferences/asset_138142_75.jsp.

Jones Lang Lasalle. 2008. *India 30: Real estate opportunities in Tier III cities*.
Retrieved     from     https://www.joneslanglasalle.com/ResearchLevel2/
JLL_WWC_India30_December_2008.pdf.

Justice, C., S. Lepeak, and A. Sundaram. 2007. Assessing the role of captive
operations in global service delivery models [white paper]. Retrieved from
http://hosteddocs.ittoolbox.com/cjsl020209.pdf.

Kaka, N. 2006, Summer. Running a customer service center in India: An
interview with the head of operations of Dell India. *McKinsey on IT*. Retrieved
from     http://www.mckinsey.com/clientservice/bto/pointofview/pdf/
MoIT8_Dell_F.pdf.

Kotabe, M. 1990. The relationship between offshore sourcing and innova-
tiveness of US multinational firms: An empirical investigation. *Journal of
International Business Studies* 21 (4):623–638.

Kotlarsky, J., and I. Oshri. 2008. Country attractiveness for offshoring and
offshore-outsourcing. *Journal of Information Technology* 23 (4):228–231.

Kurian, B., and P. P. Thimmaya. 2008, June 20. Wal-Mart plans IT back office
in Bangalore. *Economic Times*. Retrieved from http://economictimes.
indiatimes.com/Infotech/Wal-Mart_plans_IT_back_office_in_Bangalore/
articleshow/3147067.cms.

Lampel, J., and A. Bhalla. 2008. Embracing realism and recognizing choice in IT offshoring initiatives. *Business Horizons* 51:429–440.

Levina, N. 2006, December 1. In or out in an offshore context: The choice between captive centers and third-party vendors. *Cutter IT Journal*, 24–28. Retrieved from http://www.cutter.com/content/itjournal/fulltext/2006/12/itj0612d.html.

Lewin, A. Y., and C. Peeters. 2006. Offshoring work: Business hype or the onset of fundamental transformation? *Long Range Planning* 39:221–239.

A look at captive offshoring. 2008. *Offshoring Times*. Retrieved from http://www.offshoringtimes.com/Pages/2008/offshore_news1889.html.

Martin, R. 2007. India retains the offshore outsourcing crown. *Offshoring Times*. Retrieved from http://www.offshoringtimes.com/Pages/2007/offshore_news1839.html.

Maskell, P., T. Pedersen, B. Petersen, and J. Dick-Nielsen. 2006. Learning paths to offshore outsourcing: From cost reduction to knowledge seeking. Unpublished working paper. Copenhagen: Copenhagen Business School.

McCue, A. 2006. HSBC ramps up Indian presence. Retrieved from http://www.zdnetasia.com/news/business/0,39044229,61970344,00.htm.

McDougall, P. 2005. Offshoring will remain strong for India's big four. *Information Week Online*. Retrieved from http://www.informationweek.com/showArticle.jhtml?articleID=20900333&fb=20040615_software.

McFarlan, F. W., and R. L. Nolan. 1995, Winter. How to manage an IT outsourcing alliance. *Sloan Management Review*: 9–23.

Menezes, J. P. 2007. Captive centre outsourcing option not so captivating. Retrieved from http://www.itbusiness.ca/it/client/en/Home/News.asp?id=46300&bSearch=True.

Menon, M. 2005, Spring. A strategic decision framework for offshoring IT services. *Journal of Global Business*, 89–95.

Merchant, K. A. 2005. Indian BPOs curry favour. [Online] *Financial Times* (North American Edition). Retrieved from http://www.accessmylibrary.com/coms2/summary_0286-11549171_ITM.

Mishra, P. 2007, June 15. Outsourcing sees mix and match with captives, third party vendors. *Wall Street Journal*. Retrieved from http://www.livemint.com/2007/06/15003046/Outsourcing-sees-mix-and-match.html.

Mukherjee, A. 2007. India may soon boot out as a BPO-perfect nation. Retrieved from http://www.indiaresource.org/news/2007/1040.html.

Murali, D. 2005. Life cycle of a captive BPO. *Hindu Business Line*. Retrieved from http://www.thehindubusinessline.com/ew/2005/02/19/stories/2005091900300400.

Nair, P. 2008, July 8. The risk and benefits of outsourcing. *Pharma-Mag*, pp. 28–30.

NASSCOM-McKinsey. 2005. *NASSCOM-McKinsey report 2005: Extending India's leadership of the global IT and BPO industries*. Bangalore. Retrieved from http://www.mckinsey.com/locations/india/mckinseyonindia/pdf/NASSCOM_McKinsey_Report_2005.pdf.

Offshore outsourcing: Can this captive center be saved. 2007. *CIO*. Retrieved from http://www.cio.de/news/cio_worldnews/845385/index.html.

Oshri, I., and J. Kotlarsky. 2009. *Realizing the real benefits of outsourcing: Seven steps to effective outsourcing measurement*. Coventry: Warwick Business School. Retrieved from http://www.quantifyingoutsourcingbenefits.com/downloads/WBS_report-021209.pdf.

Oshri, I., J. Kotlarsky, and C. M. Liew. 2008, May 12. Four strategies for "offshore" captive centers. *Wall Street Journal*, R4.

Oshri, I., J. Kotlarsky, J. W. Rottman, and L. Willcocks. 2009. Global outsourcing: Recent trends and issues. *Information Technology & People* 22 (3):192–200.

Oshri, I., J. Kotlarsky, and L. Willcocks. 2009. *The handbook of global outsourcing and offshoring*. London: Palgrave.

Overby, S. 2006. *Global outsourcing guide*. Retrieved from http://www.cio.com/archive/071506/2006_global_outsourcing_guide.pdf.

Overby, S. 2007. Offshore outsourcing: Can this captive center be saved? *CIO*. Retrieved from http://www.cio.com/article/152701/Offshore_Outsourcing_Can_This_Captive_Center_Be_Saved_.

Palmisano, S. J. 2006. The globally integrated enterprise. *Foreign Affairs (Council on Foreign Relations)* 85 (3):127–136.

Pfannenstein, L., and R. Tsai. 2004. Offshore outsourcing: current and future effects on American IT industry. *Information Systems Management* 21 (4):72–80.

Press Trust of India. 2007, July 15. Royal Bank of Scotland to double India headcount. *Hindustantimes*. Retrieved from http://www.hindustantimes .com/News-Feed/businessbankinginsurance/Royal-Bank-of-Scotland-to -double-India-headcount/Article1-236706.aspx.

Preston, S. 2004. Lost in migration: Offshore need does not mean outsourced. *Strategy and Leadership* 32 (6):32–36.

Preston, S. 2005. Being busy abroad yourself could be best. *Human Resource Management International Digest* 13 (3):13–14.

Rajeevan, M., S. Manish, P. Beligere, and R. Williams. 2007. *Research study of captives in India and China: A majority of parent organizations also rely on third-party relationships* [white paper]. Retrieved from http://www. infosys.com/global-sourcing/white-papers/documents/captives-research -study.pdf.

Ravichandran, R., and N. Ahmed. 1993. Offshore systems development. *Information & Management* 24 (1):33–40.

Robert Bosch to set up centre in Coimbatore. 2009. *Hindu Business Line*. Retrieved from http://www.thehindubusinessline.com/2009/09/01/ stories/2009090150950200.htm.

Ross, D. 2007, September 20. Captive carve outs. Retrieved from http:// www.globalservicesmedia.com/content/general200709182883.asp.

Shivapriya, N. 2007. Captive BPO centers begin to pay off. *India Times*. Retrieved from http://economictimes.indiatimes.com/InfoTech/ITeS/ Captive_BPO_centers_begin_to_pay_off/articleshow/2402877.cms.

Siemens CEO Klaus Kleinfeld. 2006. Nobody's perfect but a team can be. *Knowledge@Wharton*. Retrieved from http://knowledge.wharton.upenn .edu/article.cfm?articleid=1447.

Steele, J. 2007. The outlook on outsourcing. *Wide Format Imaging* 15 (11):16.

Subramanian, M., and B. Atri. 2006. Captives in India: A research study. Retrieved from http://www.infosys.com/global-sourcing/white-papers/ captives-research-v2.pdf.

Tafti, M. 2005. Risk factors associated with offshore IT outsourcing. *Industrial Management & Data Systems* 105 (5):549–560.

Tholons. 2008. *Top 50 global emerging cities*. Bangalore: Tholons.

Vashistha, A., and A. Vashistha. 2006. *The offshore nation: Strategies for success in global outsourcing and offshoring*. New York: McGraw-Hill.

Vedala, S. 2008. Ten steps to setting up a captive offshore service centre. *Equaterra*. Retrieved from http://www.equaterra.com/_filelib/ FileCabinet/News/EquaTerra_Article_Setting_Up_Captive_Offshore _Svc_Ctr_Nov2007_3021EU.pdf?FileName=EquaTerra_Article_Setting_Up _Captive_Offshore_Svc_Ctr_Nov2007_3021EU.pdf.

Willcocks, L., C. Griffiths, and J. Kotlarsky. 2009. *Beyond BRIC. Offshoring in non-BRIC countries: Egypt—a new growth market*. London: London School of Economics.

Zinnov Consultancy Management. 2008. *Strategic guide on Indian R&D centers 2008*. Retrieved from http://www.zinnov.com/.

# Index